Beginning CareKit Development

Develop CareKit Applications Using Swift

Christopher Baxter

Apress®

Beginning CareKit Development

Christopher Baxter
North Yorkshire
United Kingdom

ISBN-13 (pbk): 978-1-4842-2225-6   ISBN-13 (electronic): 978-1-4842-2226-3
DOI 10.1007/978-1-4842-2226-3

Library of Congress Control Number: 2016959390

Managing Director: Welmoed Spahr
Lead Editor: Aaron Black
Technical Reviewer: Idriss Juhoor
Editorial Board: Steve Anglin, Pramila Balan, Laura Berendson, Aaron Black, Louise Corrigan, Jonathan Gennick, Robert Hutchinson, Celestin Suresh John, Nikhil Karkal, James Markham, Susan McDermott, Matthew Moodie, Natalie Pao, Gwenan Spearing
Coordinating Editor: Jessica Vakili
Copy Editor: Corbin Collins
Compositor: SPi Global
Indexer: SPi Global
Artist: SPi Global

Distributed to the book trade worldwide by Springer Science+Business Media New York, 233 Spring Street, 6th Floor, New York, NY 10013. Phone 1-800-SPRINGER, fax (201) 348-4505, e-mail orders-ny@springer-sbm.com, or visit www.springeronline.com. Apress Media, LLC is a California LLC and the sole member (owner) is Springer Science + Business Media Finance Inc (SSBM Finance Inc). SSBM Finance Inc is a Delaware corporation.

For information on translations, please e-mail rights@apress.com, or visit www.apress.com.

Apress and friends of ED books may be purchased in bulk for academic, corporate, or promotional use. eBook versions and licenses are also available for most titles. For more information, reference our Special Bulk Sales–eBook Licensing web page at www.apress.com/bulk-sales.

Any source code or other supplementary materials referenced by the author in this text are available to readers at www.apress.com. For detailed information about how to locate your book's source code, go to www.apress.com/source-code/. Readers can also access source code at SpringerLink in the Supplementary Material section for each chapter.

Printed on acid-free paper

*I'd like to dedicate this book to my gorgeous wife, Melanie,
and my amazing children, Jason and Holly, who mean everything to me.*

Contents at a Glance

Contents

About the Author

Christopher Baxter has vast experience in creating mobile apps, and has been the lead iOS engineer and architect on more than 50 apps in a wide variety of industries. With over 26 years experience in software development, Chris has been working with iOS since its first publication in 2008, as well as with the Android platform and Windows Phone. He is also the founder and director of a mobile consultancy based in the UK. He can be reached via his consultancy business at www.catalystmobile.co.

About the Technical Reviewer

Idriss Juhoor is a world-travelling software engineer from a small island in the middle of the Indian Ocean. He's worked for both small startups and large companies in different parts of the globe and now focuses on mobile healthcare. When he's not writing health apps, he's connecting stuff to his phone using solder and Bluetooth chips. You can find him on twitter: @foiegras33.

Acknowledgments

This book would not be possible without the existence of Apple and its new language Swift, which inspired me to write it.

I'd like to express my gratitude to Apress for publishing this book and to the following editors, who have put a lot of energy into making this a great book: Aaron Black, Jessica Vakii, and James Markham.

I'd also like to thank Idriss Juhoor, who has been the technical reviewer for the book. He is a keen advocate of applying good engineering practices to software projects and is involved in the digital healthcare sector.

Lastly, I'd like to thank my close friend Tom Gleeson who set the barrier for success so high I had to raise my game and write a book.

Introduction

Welcome to *Beginning CareKit Development*. My goal is to provide a practical guide for developers to create CareKit-based applications using the Swift language.

I've started with the basics, using a step-by-step approach to learning all aspects of creating a CareKit iOS application that could serve as the basis for a digital patient Care Plan. You'll see the key modules and concepts of CareKit, starting off by installing and building the open source framework.

Examples within demonstrate how to customize CareKit modules and integrate them with other frameworks, such as ResearchKit and HealthKit, and how to extend the application with Today extensions and an Apple Watch app.

By the end of the book you'll to be able to fully utilize CareKit for your own personal Care Plans. This is the future of patient care: health-tracking apps that put patients in control of their day-to-day care.

CHAPTER 1

■ ■ ■

Getting Started

This chapter introduces you to Apple's CareKit. After some background on CareKit's base classes and modules and the example app, we'll then move on to gain an understanding of how the framework is organized, the architecture of the CareKit framework, and the anatomy and key modules provided within the framework, along with some best practices for working with it.

Understanding the Core Elements of CareKit

CareKit was first introduced by Apple at a media event in March 2016. It's an open source framework that enables developers to build apps that "empower people to take on an active role in their care." iPhone apps that support this framework allow users to track their ongoing condition, symptoms, and medication to get an overall wider view of their health and share this with their care team or personal contacts. CareKit can support a wide range of care plans—from managing chronic illnesses to recovery programs after injury or surgery, and general care plans to improve health.

The CareKit framework was released as open source on April 29, 2016, and is accompanied by four example applications. The following apps are all available on the App Store and showcase the core features of CareKit, demonstrating real-world digital patient care:

- *One Drop* is for managing diabetes. It helps you track your food and medication intake, as well as activity. There's an Apple Watch app, too.

- *Start* covers the monitoring, treatment, and medication of depression, helping to diagnose mental health problems and track progress of the treatments.

Electronic supplementary material The online version of this chapter (doi:10.1007/978-1-4842-2226-3_1) contains supplementary material, which is available to authorized users.

C. Baxter, *Beginning CareKit Development*, DOI 10.1007/978-1-4842-2226-3_1

- *Glow Nurture* is a pregnancy tracker. It helps you track all the important milestones within a pregnancy, such as due dates, doctor's appointments, and so on, and also allows you to enter symptoms and measurements such as weight.

- *Glow Baby* is made by the same company as Glow Nurture, taking up the mantle after the baby is born. It covers breastfeeding, sleep, feeding, and diaper cycles.

You can see that the four sample applications are very different from each other, although they share the same underlying anatomy and structure that all CareKit apps do. In some cases, the CareKit integration is just one part of the care plan, which might include a broader set of features.

CareKit applications can be customized beyond the basic appearance of the standard module controllers provided within CareKit. We talk more about this in Chapter 4.

Apple has open sourced CareKit, and the source code comes with one example application called OCKSample, which demonstrates all the key models within CareKit.

Links to the source code, documentation, and other information can be found on www.apple.com/researchkit/ and www.carekit.org. The source code is hosted on Github at https://github.com/carekit-apple.

Fundamentally, CareKit manages various scenes for scheduling patient activities, monitoring treatment, and providing feedback to the patient and their connections. You can find an overview of these modules and the key data classes in the official documentation. If you've already read the documentation, you may want to skip to the "CareKit Framework Architecture" section.

Framework Organization

There are six modules in CareKit. Four relate to providing the user interface, and two are for managing data.

User interface modules:

- Care Card

- Symptom and Measurement Tracker

- Insights

- Connect

Data modules:

- Care Plan Store

- Documents Exporter

As you will see, generally most CareKit classes are easily recognizable as they are prefixed with OCK. We can now take a closer look at each module.

User Interface Modules

CareKit provides a number of ViewController-derived objects that take care of loading the appropriate data and presenting it to the user. Each ViewController interacts with the Care Plan Store and various key data objects that represent the care plan.

Care Card

The Care Card manages intervention activities that a user needs to perform as part of the treatment for their condition. The Care Card is a scene managed by the OCKCareCardViewController object and presents the intervention activities to the user. Intervention activities are basically scheduled tasks that the user must perform as part of their treatment—for example, taking medication three times a day.

You can read more about the Care Card scene and what it's used for in the official documentation. Chazpter 4 covers creating, presenting, and interacting with the Care Card view.

Figure 1-1 shows a typical Care Card ViewController.

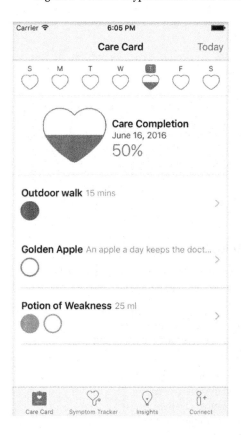

Figure 1-1. *Care Card ViewController*

Figure 1-2 shows the detail view for a specific intervention activity.

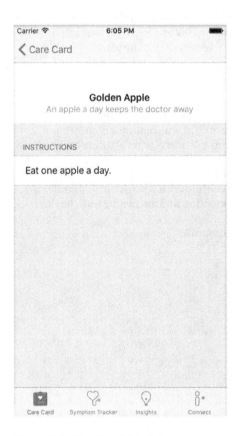

Figure 1-2. *Care Card detail view*

Symptom and Measurement Tracker

The Symptom and Measurement Tracker manages activities that are used to evaluate the effectiveness of the treatments. There are two types of these activities:

- *Subjective activities* allow users to record symptoms like their mood or pain scales. You as the developer can implement your own tasks to record these symptoms or integrate with existing tasks provided through ResearchKit.

- *Objective activities* are measurements that can be entered manually or recorded from devices or even HealthKit—for example, blood pressure. The Symptom and Measurement Tracker scene is managed by the OCKSymptomTrackerViewController.

More details on the Symptom and Measurement Tracker scene can be found on the official documentation site too. I'll be covering how to present and interact with the scene using ResearchKit, and in Chapter 5 how to develop your own custom task views. Figure 1-3 shows a typical Symptom and Measurement ViewController.

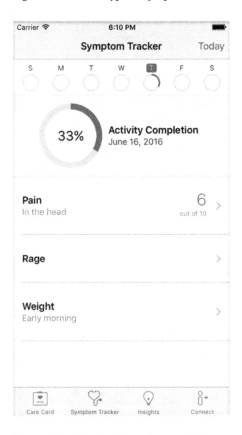

Figure 1-3. *A typical Symptom and Measurement ViewController*

Figure 1-4 shows an activity task view prompting the user to choose a scaled value.

Figure 1-4. *An activity task view*

Insights

Insights display charts and messages to inform the user on the progress of their Care Plan. The CareKit framework provides two types of views for this: chart views and messages.

There is just one chart type provided by CareKit: a horizontal bar chart. This chart enables a user to visualize the correlation between a treatment's intervention activities and the assessment activities.

A good example of an insight might be to view a chart that compares the users daily pain scales to the recorded medication they've taken. One could extend this to data recorded in a survey from other patients too, potentially by integrating ResearchKit into the application (more about this later).

Messages can also be displayed to the user to provide tips or alerts to help the user stay on track with their health goals. Potentially this might also integrate in with a broader solution that allows doctors or other members of the care team to communicate information about treatment updates to the patient.

The Insights scene is managed by the OCKInsightsViewController and you can read a little more detail about this on the official documentation site. Later chapters cover the implementation to present and interact with the Insight view.

■ **Note** Charts and messages are not restricted to CareKit data; any arbitrary data can be displayed. In Figure 1-5, there is a single message insight and a chart insight that compare the values of Head Pain to the related Medication Adherence.

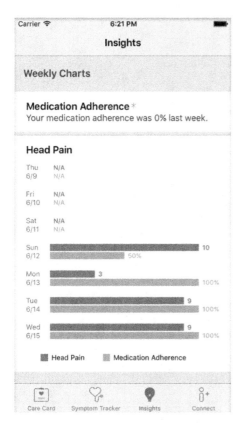

Figure 1-5. Typical Insights dashboard

Connect

Connect is a scene that helps a user communicate and share their progress and Insights with their Care Team and personal connections such as family and friends. This module displays a list of connections. The user can select a connection and choose to call or email the selected person as well as send them a report or an attachment of photos or documents.

The Connect scene is managed by the OCKConnectViewController and again more details can be found on the official document. Our focus will remain on how to present and interact with the Connect scene and how to populate it with connection data. Figure 1-6 displays details of a typical Care Team. which may include carers and also friends and family.

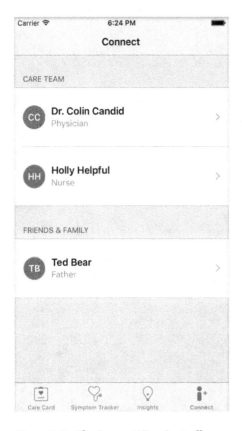

Figure 1-6. *The Connect ViewController*

When a specific connection is selected, the details view is presented as shown in Figure 1-7.

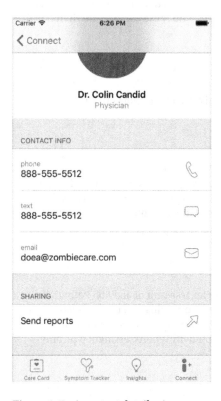

Figure 1-7. *A contact details view*

Data Modules

CareKit provides a number of modules to handle all the data for your Care Plan.

Care Plan Store

CareKit has a persistent database that stores the data used by the Care Card and Symptom and Measurement Tracker and Insights scenes.

This store is not accessible directly, but only through the OCKPlanStore object. CareKit will automatically load the store data when it is created and save any changes.

Under the hood, CareKit uses CoreData backed with a NSSQLiteStoreType data store which is secured using NSFileProtectionComplete.

We'll delve deeper into the workings of the Care Plan Store in Chapter 3 to see how to use it and discuss its relation to various key data types.

Documents Exporter

An OCKDocument object is used to create reports with insight data. It can create reports as PDF or HTML which include text, charts, and images, and these can then be shared with connections.

Key Data Types

The key modules and objects just reviewed depend on a few key data objects for storing and managing data.

Intervention Activity

The OCKCarePlanActivity object is used to represent an intervention activity. Typically, multiple intervention activities make up a user's Care Plan. These activities are defined with the OCKCarePlanActivityTypeIntervention type and are stored in the Care Plan Store to be used by the Care Card.

Assessment Activity

The OCKCarePlanActivity is also used to represent an assessment activity. Potentially, there will be multiple assessment activities used for monitoring and evaluating the patient treatment, and these will be displayed in the Symptom and Measurement Tracker. These activities are defined with the OCKCarePlanActivityTypeAssessment type and again are stored in the Care Plan Store.

Intervention Event

An intervention event is a scheduled task that a user is expected to perform in association with the intervention activity. CareKit will generate one or more OCKCarePlanEvent objects related to an active activity. For example, if there is an activity to take some medication three times a day, then CareKit will generate three events for each day. Events have a completion status.

Assessment Event

An assessment event is a scheduled task that a user is expected to perform in association with an assessment activity. CareKit will generate one or more OCKCarePlanEvent objects related to an active assessment activity. For example, if there is an activity to monitor pain once a day, CareKit will generate one event for each day. Developers will be responsible for creating an OCKCarePlanEventResult to record the result of an assessment task.

Contact

An OCKContact object represents a contact being displayed in the Contacts module.

Chart

A concrete OCKChart subclass is used to create the visual representation of the Care Plan data in the Insights module.

CareKit Framework Architecture

Before expanding on details of how these CareKit modules fit within an application, let's have a quick overview of the overall architecture of the CareKit framework to better understand the responsibilities and relationships between the core classes and objects.

To begin with, we'll see a logical design of the overall CareKit framework and then drill down into some specifics on the presentation and data layers, as presented in Figure 1-8.

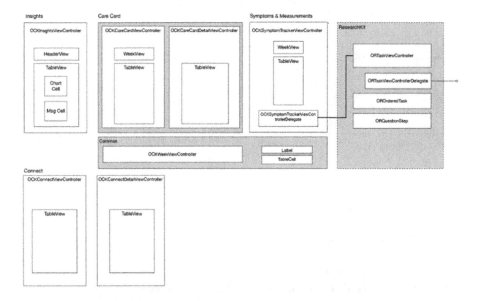

Figure 1-8. *Logical overview*

If we take a high-level view of the layers within the framework, we can see this is divided into two key layers that represent the classes and data types described earlier in the chapter: the presentation layer and the data layer.

It's worth noting that CareKit has a dependency on the HealthKit framework too. CareKit event results can be based on HealthKit Samples, Correlation, and Category types.

The data layer also has a dependency on CoreData, which it uses for persistence.

Presentation Layer

Figure 1-9 takes a look at the presentation layer in more detail.

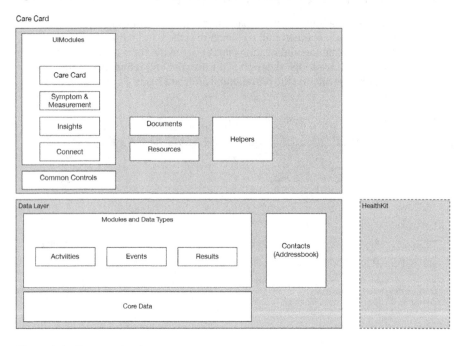

Figure 1-9. *Presentation layer*

We can see that each of the main scenes in CareKit is represented by a ViewController, and each ViewController is rendering data through a number of different controls, including some customer headers and standard table views. The Care Plan and Symptom and Measurement Tracker ViewControllers also share a week ViewController. Here are a few pointers to take along the way:

- The OCKCareCardViewController and OCKSymptomTrackerViewController both implement a single PageController, which in this case is the OCKWeekViewController within common controls.

- Whereas OCKCareCardViewController and
  OCKConnectViewController have their own respective detail
  ViewControllers, the OCKSymptomTrackerViewController
  provides the OCKSymptomTrackerViewControllerDelegate,
  which must be implemented by the developer. The
  CareKit sample application OCKSample demonstrates
  this by integrating with ResearchKit to present a single
  step task using ORKQuestionStep, ORKOrderedTask, and
  ORKTaskViewController. The host application in this case handles
  the ORKTaskViewControllerDelegate when a task is completed.
  You can, of course, implement and present your own assessment
  tasks if required.

We'll see and implement these classes in detail when constructing our own sample application in later chapters.

Data Layer

To support the presentation, we have the data layer, outlined in Figure 1-10.

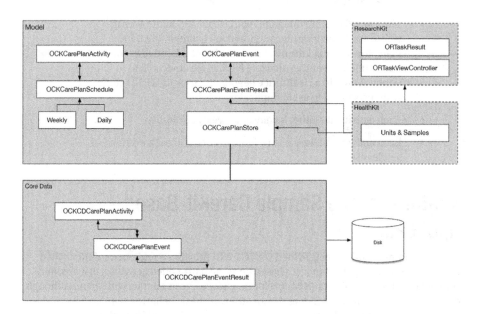

Figure 1-10. *Architecture data layer*

You'll see more details about the classes in the data layer in Chapter 3 when we discuss the Care Plan Store in detail. For now, it's sufficient to understand the basic relationship between the key types:

- Developers do not access the CareKit database directly. All interaction is done through the Care Plan Store, which provides all the CRUD methods for activities, events, and results. More specifically, it handles the following:

  - Storing and deleting activities

  - Setting an activity's end date

  - Reading activities and events

  - Creating and updating events

- Classes named with the CD acronym represent the internal CoreData–managed objects and relationships for activities, events, and event results, that is, OCKCDCarePlanActivity, OCKCDCarePlanEvent, and OCKCDCarePlanEventResult. The Care Plan Store object implements all CoreData functionality and is backed by a SQL Store with NSSQLiteStoreType type.

- The Care Plan Store integrates with HealthKit. In the scenario where assessment results are stored in Healthkit, the Care Plan Store can load results from HealthKit and initialize an OCKCarePlanEventResult using HKSample objects. This is implemented in a HealthKit category and uses the UUID stored with the sample to avoid duplicates.

- Each activity has either a daily or a weekly schedule.

- Each activity can have one or more events, and each event has a single result.

Anatomy of the Sample CareKit-Based Application

The OCKSample application provided with CareKit provides a reference solution when developing CareKit applications. It's based on some hard-coded activities, insights, and connections that use the default controllers to allow users to interact with them. Although simple and a little contrived, it does demonstrate the basic behavior of a CareKit application and includes some integration with ResearchKit and HealthKit.

Readers should note, though, that a real-world application using CareKit is more likely to have a broader set of features, some customization, and back-end support and be related to a specific treatment or Care Plan.

In this section we'll delve into the design and architecture of the sample application, which will give you some further practical insight into how to use and integrate CareKit.

Application Design

OCKSample is a tab-based application which uses a separate tab for each default CareKit controller: Care Card tab, Symptom and Measurement tab, Insights tab, and Connect Tab.

The application does not actually specify treatment for a particular illness or health problem; rather, it presents a few hard-coded activities, assessment tasks, and contacts.

Application Architecture

The application consists of the following key components:

- In the presentation layer we have a UITabController called RootViewController, which creates and instantiates the four main CareKit controllers, placing each one in a NavigationController.

- The data layer consists of numerous concrete activity classes and an extension protocol. There's a factory class for creating insights and a couple of NSOperations to handle asynchronous activity event queries, and lastly a singleton class that provides a wrapper to the Care Plan Store.

- We also have a SampleData class, which represents some sample data.

The other classes include some extensions, helpers, standard UIKit and Foundation classes, and storyboard.

Controllers

RootViewController is a standard implementation of UITabViewController and adds the default CareKit Controllers. It creates the CarePlanStoreManager singleton, which it stores a reference property to and which is used to pass a reference to the Care Plan Store to the controllers when instantiated. It also creates the SampleData object. Lastly, the RootViewController also implements two delegates.

The OCKSymptomTrackerViewControllerDelegate provides the didSelectRowWithAssessmentEvent(...) method, which, as its name indicates, is used to handle the event when a user selects an assessment activity in the Symptom and Measurement Tracker view. This delegate method is used to look up the activity type, return the activity object from the sample data, and, if the assessment event has not been completed, create a ResearchKit ORTaskViewController, which is pushed onto the stack.

The main thing to notice here is that the activity itself is responsible for creating the ResearchKit task using the task() method. This then also has a dependency on HealthKit types.

The RootViewController also conforms to the ORKTaskViewControllerDelegate and implements the didFinishWithReason(...) method. The purpose of this implementation is to handle the completion of an activity assessment as presented earlier. In this case, the implementation will create an OCKCarePlanEventResult object. The result is then converted to a HealthKit sample and stored in the HealthKit database or, failing that, stored in the CareKit Care Plan Store.

15

CareStorePlanManager

The CareStorePlanManager is a singleton. It creates the CareKit Store (OCKPlanStore) and handles its delegate events. It's also responsible for building insights, based on the data in the store. All interaction with the Care Plan Store is done through the CareStorePlanManager.

The CareStorePlanManager then implements the two methods from OCKCarePlanStoreDelegate, which are used to update insights when an activity is changed or updated in the stores database.

Finally, the CareStorePlanManager defines its own CarePlanStoreManagerDelegate, which is used to notify delegate handlers when insights have been updated. This delegate is actually only handled by the RootViewController, which in turn updates the InsightsViewController items property.

This basically outlines the anatomy of the sample application. As you can see, there is literally no UI custom coding required, as it's all handled by the default CareKit ViewControllers. The sample app simply coordinates the provisioning of some sample activities and displays for the ViewControllers, handling a few updates, and leaves the responsibility of UI updates to the Care Plan Store and the default controllers.

Best Practices

The CareKit framework uses a local data store but does not integrate with any remote servers. Developers will need to write their own code to transmit and store data on a remote server as part of a wider solution. You can choose to use any data solution you like, but care should be taken to ensure data privacy and security.

Privacy

Patient privacy is a core principal within the healthcare industry. Medical apps must ensure the highest level of security to maintain the privacy of one's data. The following principals should be followed:

- Have a privacy policy. Note this will be enforced for CareKit apps that are posted on the App Store.

- Use touch ID or PIN access to control access to an app.

- Do not store data in iCloud.

Security

Although privacy protects access to users' data, there is also data security to consider. Developers should do the following:

- *Use the highest levels of file protection.* On iOS this can be achieved by using the iOS NSFileProtectionComplete or NSFileProtectionCompleteUnlessOpen APIs. These ensure that all stored data is encrypted automatically.

- *Consider a cryptographic wrapper to protect data in transit.* For example, a Cryptographic Message Syntax (CMS) envelope can be used to encrypt data before transmitting.

- *Transmit data only over SSL.*

Accessibility

Apple recommend that all CareKit applications should follow a minimum set of rules when adding new user interface elements to the open source CareKit framework, including the following:

- All UI elements should be reachable with VoiceOver enabled and have proper accessibility labels.

- Add accessibility hints and traits to describe UI elements whose purposes might be difficult to describe with just a label.

- Actions such as tapping, swiping, and other interaction with UI elements should be possible to perform with VoiceOver enabled.

- When possible, follow the accessibility conventions and patterns embraced by Apple's own apps.

Summary

This chapter has outlined the core modules and data types that are used in CareKit and that represent a Care Plan for a patient. You've gained a deeper understanding of the architecture of the CareKit framework and its integrations with ResearchKit and HealthKit. You've also seen that CareKit has its own CoreData store, which is held locally on the device, noting that developers will need to build their own back-end server for a broader solution. Lastly, I gave you an overview of the sample application provided with the CareKit source demonstrating how the core components are used together. As with all healthcare applications, data privacy and security are essential considerations, and care should be taken to follow these best practices.

In the next chapter we will work together setting up a simple Hello World app to demonstrate how to integrate CareKit into your project.

CHAPTER 2

■ ■ ■

CareKit Hello World

In this chapter, we will be creating a simple Hello World app using CareKit. You will learn how to integrate CareKit, alongside ResearchKit and HealthKit, into your Xcode project, as well as configure the project with data protection.

I will present the Care Card controller with one simple Hello World task using ResearchKit to demonstrate that the integration is working. At the end of the chapter I'll introduce you to the fun sample application: a care plan for the Zombie Virus (as it's fairly current these days) called the ZombieCare app.

Let's get started and build the Hello World app.

Create the Workspace and Project

Prepare your project workspace by doing the following:

1. In the folder of your choice (I use /Users/user_name/ Development/mobile), create a new folder called carebook (that is, `mkdir carebook`).

2. `cd` in the folder using the command `cd /Users/user_name/ development/mobile/carebook` , substituting your own project root folder.

3. Note that we will be using Xcode 7.3.1 and Swift 2.2. Open Xcode and select File ➤ New ➤ Workspace. You will be presented with a dialog. Change to your carebook project folder and enter your workspace name as `CareKitBook`.

These next steps demonstrate how to add a simple Xcode application to your workspace:

1. With the Xcode workspace open, click the + button from the bottom left of the project navigator and select New Project.

2. Now select the Single View Application template and click Next, as demonstrated in Figure 2-1.

© Christopher Baxter 2016
C. Baxter, *Beginning CareKit Development*, DOI 10.1007/978-1-4842-2226-3_2

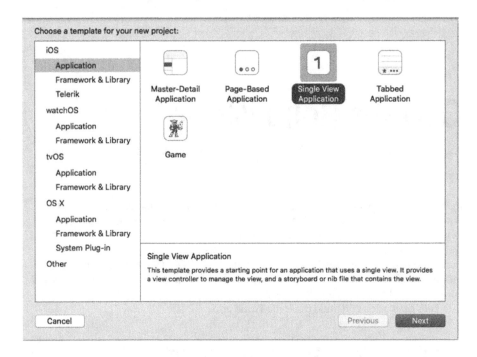

Figure 2-1. *New project*

3. Create a new HelloWorldCK project using the settings as shown in the project properties dialog in Figure 2-2.

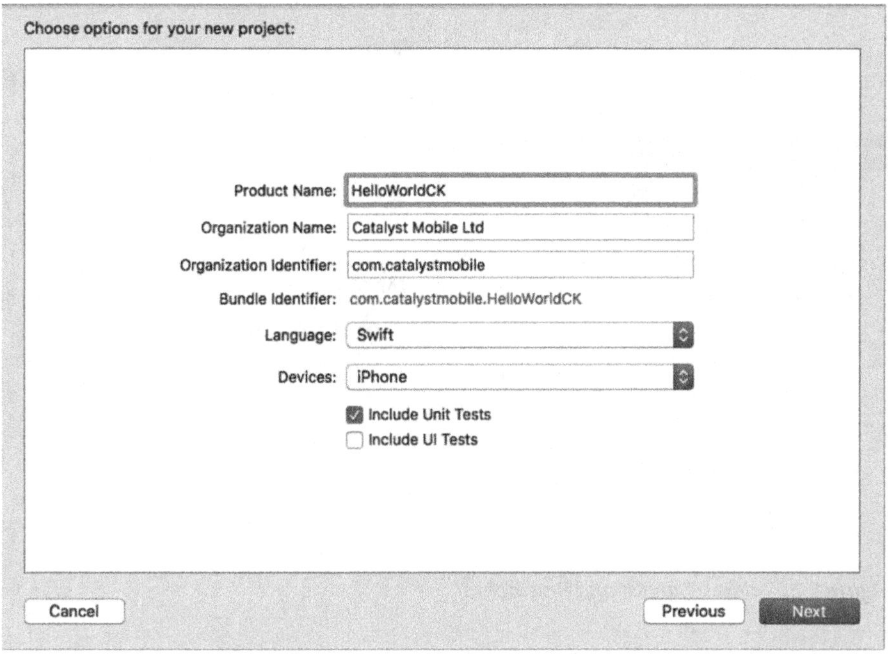

```
Choose options for your new project:

              Product Name:  HelloWorldCK

          Organization Name:  Catalyst Mobile Ltd

       Organization Identifier:  com.catalystmobile

          Bundle Identifier:  com.catalystmobile.HelloWorldCK

                  Language:  Swift

                   Devices:  iPhone

                            ☑ Include Unit Tests
                            ☐ Include UI Tests



    Cancel                              Previous     Next
```

Figure 2-2. *Project settings*

Import CareKit and ResearchKit

You will now add the CareKit open source framework along with ResearchKit and verify that the application builds okay:

1. Switch to the terminal app and cd into the /Users/user_name/ development/mobile/carebook folder you created earlier.

2. Run the following command to download the latest stable build of CareKit and its dependencies. This will create a subfolder in your project folder called carekit.

   ```
   git clone -b stable --recurse-submodules
   https://github.com/carekit-apple/carekit.git
   ```

3. Drag and drop CareKit.xcodeproj from the newly cloned carekit folder into your HelloWorkCK project, as depicted in Figure 2-3. Then repeat the same for ResearchKit.xcodeproj, which is in the /carekit/dependency folder.

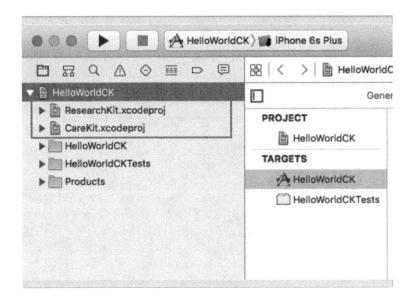

Figure 2-3. *Adding CareKit and ResearchKit*

4. Now embed the framework libraries into your project as
   dynamic frameworks. Select the top level HelloWorldCK
   project in your workspace and ensure the General tab is
   selected. Use the + button in the Embedded Binaries section
   to add both the ResearchKit and CareKit iOS frameworks, as
   demonstrated in Figure 2-4.

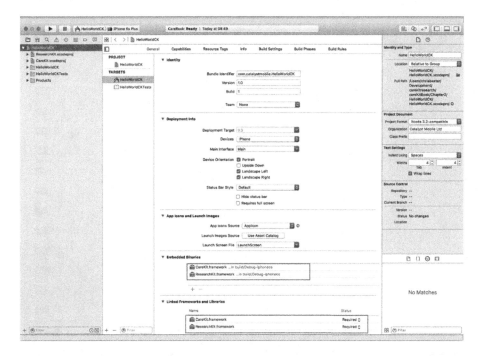

Figure 2-4. *Including libraries*

Your HelloWorldCK app is now ready to build. Press Command+B to build the app. The absence of build errors indicates successful integration of ResearchKit in the project.

■ **Note** You can also import ResearchKit and CareKit in your project using the dependency manager such as Cocoapods or Carthage. It's likely that there will also be support in Swift3 with the Swift Package Manager, so keep a look out for that in the future.

Configure the Project with Data Protection

As mentioned earlier, privacy and data protection are both very important for healthcare apps. We set up data protection for the app before adding any further code. By enabling Data Protection, a level of security is added to all files stored on disk by the app in the apps container. For more information, see Apple's documentation on Data Protection.

1. Select the Capabilities tab and open the section for Data Protection.

2. Turn the switch on for Data Protection, as shown in Figure 2-5. At this point you may find Xcode will prompt you to select your developer account, as Data Protection entitlements need to be added to your provisioning profile when building the application.

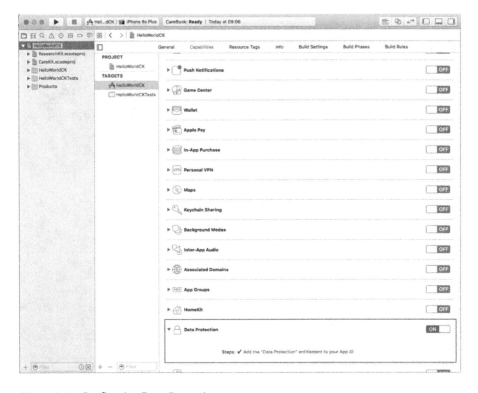

Figure 2-5. Configuring Data Protection

Hello World!

At this point we're now ready to add some basic CareKit functionality into your application. Build and run your application in the simulator to ensure it's all working by pressing Command+R on the keyboard. For now you will simply see the default single view-based application with a blank screen.

Creating a Care Card

In the next few steps we are going to create and present a simple Care Card with a single intervention activity. To achieve this we need to do the following:

1. Instantiate the app's single Care Plan Store.

2. Add our Hello World activity.

3. Present the Care Card controller and view.

First, we want to prepare our template project and default controller with a button in order to have an action we can call:

1. Open the project and select the Main.storyboard file in the project navigator. You will see the storyboard with the default View Controller Scene. Select the ViewController and from the menu, click Editor ➤ Embed In ➤ Navigation Controller.

2. Switch focus back to the ViewController and add a new button, changing the text to Show Care Card. Align the button using the auto layout constraints for Horizontal and Vertical layout in Container, as in Figure 2-6.

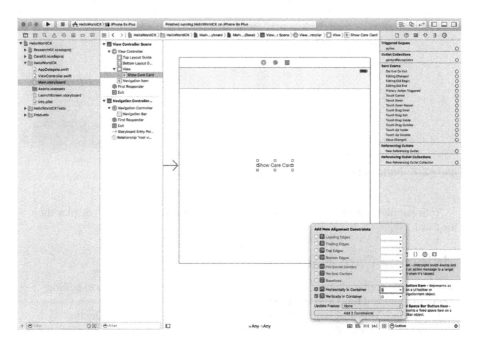

Figure 2-6. *Adding a button*

3. Next we will add the button click event handler to the default ViewController, as shown in Figure 2-7. Show the Assistant Editor by clicking the button on the toolbar with the two concentric circles. Now, while holding down the Ctrl key, drag across to the ViewController and drop the cursor within the class implementation. Enter the method name showCareCard into the dialog.

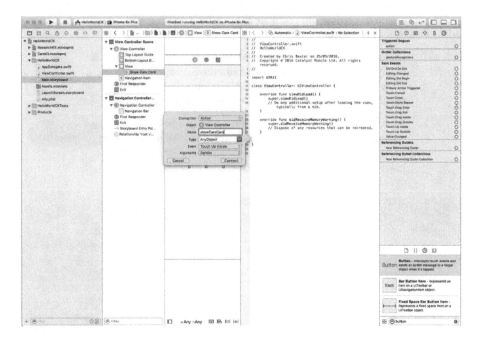

Figure 2-7. *Button handler*

Your handler is now ready. This will be where we will write our code to display the Care Card.

Adding the Care Plan Store

Now that we've prepared our Hello World project, we can take the first step to adding support for our Card Card into the application.

In the ViewController.swift file, import the CareKit framework by adding the following line at the top of the file:

```
import CareKit
```

Now add the following constant and init method to the ViewController.swift file:

```
let store: OCKCarePlanStore
required init?(coder aDecoder: NSCoder) {
// 1.
      let fileManager = NSFileManager.defaultManager()
      guard let documentDirectory =   fileManager.URLsForDirectory
      (.DocumentDirectory, inDomains: .UserDomainMask).last else {
          fatalError("*** Error: Unable to get the document directory! ***")
      }
```

```
    let storeURL = documentDirectory.URLByAppendingPathComponent
("HelloCareKitStore")
//2.
    if !fileManager.fileExistsAtPath(storeURL.path!) {
        try! fileManager.createDirectoryAtURL(storeURL,
        withIntermediateDirectories: true, attributes: nil)
    }
    //3.
    store = OCKCarePlanStore(persistenceDirectoryURL: storeURL)
    super.init(coder: aDecoder)
}
```

Here we declare a new constant to hold our Care Plan Store. You only need one Care Plan Store per app, so that's why it is a constant as it should be long-lived through the lifecycle of the app.

We then add an initializer to our controller, which does the following:

1. Generates a URL to a directory inside the apps document directory using the NSFileManager.

2. Verifies that the directory exists and if not creates it.

3. Instantiates the Care Plan Store and assigns it to the constant variable for later use. Note at this point you could assign the store's delegate too, so you can reposed to the changes in the store, but we'll come back to that later in our sample application.

Note that for this simple, contrived example, there is only some rudimentary error checking, but in a real-world application, better care should be taken to handle errors properly.

When the store is instantiated, it will automatically load any existing activities and save any further changes you make.

Adding an Intervention Activity

In the next step we will add our Hello World activity. This activity will be an intervention activity, scheduled three times a day. It tasks the user to say Hello and provides some advice on the activity details.

Add the following createActivity() function to the ViewController.swift file:

```
func createActivity() {
    //1.
    let MyMedicationIdentifier = "HelloActivity"
    //2.
     store.activityForIdentifier(MyMedicationIdentifier) { (success,
     foundActivity, error) in
```

27

```
//3.
guard success else {
        // perform real error handling here.
        fatalError("*** An error occurred \(error?.
        localizedDescription) ***")
    }
 if let activity = foundActivity {
        //activity already exists
        print("Activity found - \(activity.identifier)")
 }
 else {
 // 4.
        let startDay = NSDateComponents(year: 2016, month: 3, day: 15)
            let thriceADay = OCKCareSchedule.
            dailyScheduleWithStartDate
            (startDay, occurrencesPerDay: 3)
    //5.

            let medication = OCKCarePlanActivity(
        identifier: MyMedicationIdentifier,
        groupIdentifier: nil,
        type: .Intervention,
        title: "Hello World",
        text: "Say aloud",
        tintColor: nil,
        instructions: "Say Hello to the world 3 times a day.
        This should make you feel better. It is not recommended
        to drive with this medication. For any severe side
        effects, please contact your physician.",
        imageURL: nil,
        schedule: thriceADay,
        resultResettable: true,
        userInfo:nil)
            //6.
            self.store.addActivity(medication, completion: {
            (success, error) in guard success else {
            // perform real error handling here.
            fatalError("*** An error occurred \(error?.
            localizedDescription) ***")
        }
    })
    }
    }
}
```

The following numbered points are an explanation of the `createActivity()` function. The numbered points are displayed as comments in the code:

1. Declare a constant for activity identifier, as each activity has a unique identifier.

2. Check to see if the activity already exists in the store using the identifier. If not, then we can add the activity.

3. We place a guard statement around the success value returned to ensure that the call was successful.

4. At this point we can create the activity. Start by creating a schedule with an instance of the OCKCareSchedule class. Here we are creating a daily schedule for three occurrences per day. You should read up on the API for further options on this, including weekly schedules and schedules that skip days.

5. Finally we create an instance of an activity with OCKCarePlanActivity, passing it the schedule and identifier and setting a few other parameters, including the title, text, and some instructions.

6. The HelloWorld activity is then added to the store and we check that this is successful in the completion block.

Note that the activity object is immutable, meaning that its properties cannot be changed once it's been created. We set its activity type to .intervention. This ensures it appears in the Care Card. The properties are mandatory, including a schedule, title, text, and the instructions.

With this activity we should see that the schedule sets three circles to be filled in each day. The title and text fields will be displayed on the Care Card, and the instructions will appear in the activities detail view. The other parameters are optional. We'll go into more detail in the sample app later.

We then call the `createActivity()` method from within the ViewDidLoad:

```swift
override func viewDidLoad() {
    super.viewDidLoad()
    //Add a single hello world activity to the store
    createActivity()
    }
```

Finally, we can present the activity to the user using the Care Card ViewController as follows:

```swift
@IBAction func showCareCard(sender: AnyObject) {
    let careCardViewController = OCKCareCardViewController(carePlanSto
re: store)
// presenting the view controller modally
    self.navigationController?.pushViewController(careCardViewController,
    animated: true)
    }
}
```

In the button handler, we first instantiate the OCKCareCardViewController controller, making sure we pass the Care Plan Store to it and then push it onto the navigation controller.

From this point on, CareKit automatically updates the Care Card whenever there are changes to the Care Plan Store.

Go ahead and run the application in the simulator using Command+R. Tap on the button to show the Care Card, and you should see the screens, as shown in Figure 2-8. (Note, we've already tapped on two circles to demonstrate filling up the circles and heart.)

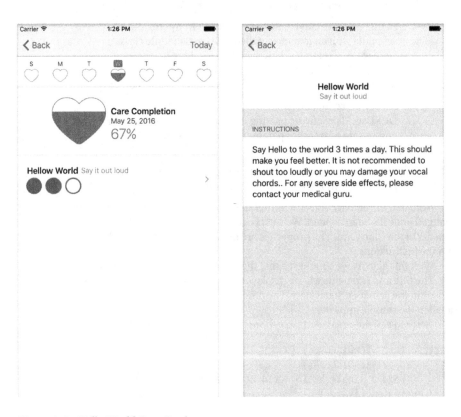

Figure 2-8. Hello World Care Card

Introducing ZombieCare

Moving forward from this chapter we will be developing on an app named ZombieCare and a Care Plan for a fictitious condition called zombification. This will keep things fun and interesting while demonstrating all the key aspects of a Care Plan, the CareKit framework modules, and integration with ResearchKit and HealthKit.

As we all know, a cure for zombification is theoretically impossible, as zombies are already dead, but that won't stop us trying. The CarePlan will include certain treatments and ways to assess the severity of the virus.

This sample app will be developed as close to a real production style app as possible, so all things will be considered including architecture, software patterns, error checking, and more.

You can find the base ZombieCare project on the Github repository. Download and open the project from within the Chapter 3 folder.

Summary

In this chapter you learned how to create a basic application and integrate CareKit along with ResearchKit frameworks into the app. You were introduced to the Care Plan Store and a single activity, which was presented in a Care Card. You also learned a little about the ZombieCare project we will be building on for the rest of the book.

In the next chapter we'll be taking a look at the Care Plan Store in more detail. We'll introduce a Store Management class and look at how to manage activities and events and respond to changes in the store.

CHAPTER 3

■ ■ ■

Care Plan Store

In this chapter we will get an in-depth look at the Care Plan Store. You will learn about the Care Plan Store and its delegates and the key data types, how data is stored and read, and how the Care Plan Store responds to changes, as well as some housekeeping such as clearing the store. This chapter also introduces a set of classes that we will use in the ZombieCare app for handling the Care Plan Store and its data.

This is a long and detailed chapter, so allow some time to read and absorb its contents.

OCKCarePlanStore

CareKit provides us with the OCKCarePlanStore object which is used to store a patient's treatment plan in what we refer to as the Care Plan Store. When activities are added to the store they are automatically saved, and the store will record the progress as treatment and assessment events are completed by the patient.

There are a number of options open to developers on how activities are created. For instance, they can be simply hard-coded into an app, like in the CareKit OCKSample application. They might be generated as a result of a survey taken by the user, or simply stored as internal resources, such as a JSON file. ResearchKit might be an option to survey the user and depending on the results, a set of activities could be created. Depending on your resources and app design, it may be that you download your patient's records or their treatment plan from a server and parse the data into activities on the app at runtime.

Once added to the store, the activities can only have their endDate updated or removed, and at runtime these changes will be reflected in the provided Care Card and Symptom and Measurement Tracker ViewControllers as they observe the Care Plan Store for changes by implementing the OCKCarePlanStoreDelegate. Any part of your app may also observe events from the Care Plan Store; I'll demonstrate this later in the chapter.

© Christopher Baxter 2016

C. Baxter, *Beginning CareKit Development*, DOI 10.1007/978-1-4842-2226-3_3

Storage

The Care Plan Store uses CoreData to create a SQLite database located at the URL specified in the initializer of the OCKPlanStore object. This is how the URL is created:

```
let searchPaths = NSSearchPathForDirectoriesInDomains
(.ApplicationSupportDirectory, .UserDomainMask, true)
let applicationSupportPath = searchPaths[0]
let persistenceDirectoryURL = NSURL(fileURLWithPath: applicationSupportPath)
if !NSFileManager.defaultManager().fileExistsAtPath(persistenceDirectoryURL.
absoluteString, isDirectory: nil) {
        try! NSFileManager.defaultManager().createDirectoryAtURL
        (persistenceDirectoryURL, withIntermediateDirectories: true,
        attributes: nil)
    }
```

You start by specifying the persistent directory URL using the application support directory. Then check if the directory exists, and if not, use the NSFileManager's createDirectoryURL() method passing the new persistenceDirectoryURL you created in the first step.

Initialization

To initialize the Care Plan Store, you instantiate an instance passing the persistenceDirectoryURL to the initializer:

```
let store = OCKCarePlanStore(persistenceDirectoryURL:
persistenceDirectoryURL)
```

The OCKPlanStore initializer will create the CoreData Managed Object Context and related CoreData objects such as the NSPersistentStoreCoordinator.

When creating the Care Plan Store instance, developers must create it on the main thread of the application, but its methods can be called from any thread within the app. Internally the Care Plan Store initializes the NSManagedObject context using the NSPrivateQueueConcurrencyType.

After initializing the Care Plan Store, all method calls work to a FIFO background queue using the NSManagedObjectContext's performBlock:^ method. As soon as the work is done, a completion handler is called on an anonymous background thread with the results. Users of the API should dispatch the results back onto the main thread. We'll demonstrate this in the ZombieCare app.

Security

When the Care Plan Store is initialized, and it creates the database, it is encrypted using standard file encryption by way of NSFileProtectionComplete as an option on the NSPersistentStoreCoordinator. This prevents data from being read or written to when a device is locked or booting.

This is all handled internally by the Care Plan Store, and though it's useful to understand, you don't have to do anything directly yourself.

Accessing the Care Plan Store

When working with CareKit data you don't access data directly. Instead the Care Plan Store provides methods to add or remove activities to the store. Once an activity has been added, only the endDate of an activity can be changed using the setEndDate:forActivity:completion method.

You can query the store to obtain the following:

- Get all the activities in the store

- Get all the activities of a given type (intervention or assessment) in the store

- Get the activity for a given identifier

- Get activities for a given group identifier

- Get the events of a type (intervention or assessment) for a given date

- Get the events for a given activity for a given date

- Enumerate all the events for a given activity for a range of dates

- Enumerate the completion status for a given type (intervention or assessment) for a range of dates

Now that you have an understanding of the Care Plan Store's role and a little insight to its inner workings, we'll work our way through a practical example that we'll add to the ZombieCare app, and we'll explain as we go along the different data types used within CareKit.

Adding to the ZombieCare App

Let's get started by opening the ZombieCare workspace and project from Chapter3_start\ZombieCare.xcworkspace.

This project already has CareKit and ResearchKit integrated using the same approach we took in Chapter 2 with the Hello World app. The ZombieCare app is based on the single view app template. In this chapter our goal will be to work through the creation of a set of activities and add them to the Care Plan Store. We're going to make this as real world as possible, because after all, we know there are Zombies about and they certainly need some treatment.

The concept behind our app is that we'll be loading a Care Plan from a mock remote resource and so emulate what we might do in a production application. In this chapter we have provided the mock Care Plan service in such a way that you can extend it with additional real services if you want to. In theory the patient using the app could feed back their insights to the care team and receive an updated Care Plan back through the service with additional messages, activities, and amendments to the Care Plan if needed.

The Care Plan will therefore be updatable and include everything we need to create scheduled activities, connections, messages, and so on, which we will implement in stages.

Setup

In the project folder, look for the file careplan.json. This file represents the ZombieCare plan in JSON format. We've included this file in the resources of the project and will load it using the MockService services. This JSON could just as easily be returned from a remote server in response to an HTTP request. In the file you will find some general fields relating to the Care Plan and a number of intervention and assessment activities. I'll explain all these fields in more detail as we load and map the data into the Care Plan Store.

You will also find a few other classes already provided that are used for loading the Care Plan and converting the JSON into some local objects that can be used by the application. This section offers a brief explanation of the classes.

The ZCService file includes the ZCServiceType and a protocol with a single method called request, which takes some generic parameters including the request resource and response. The ZCAPIResource is a request configuration that can include fields such as paths, request headers, parameters, and so on. You can customize this further if you need to have additional fields. For our mock service, we just require the paths field. The ZCAPIResponse is another simple protocol that defines the required initializer with the init?(date: NSData?).

The ZCServiceProvider file contains a helper method to allow us to load a specific service. As mentioned, we have provided just one mock service. We can request from the provider a new service of type .Mock, which will return a new instance of MockService. The MockService conforms to the ZCService protocol and therefore provides an implementation of the request method that loads the careplan.json and returns this in the completion handler. By following this pattern, making use of generics and protocols, you can implement your own ZCServiceType, which might, for example, use some networking code to load the Care Plan from a remote server.

Additional Files

There are two additional files you need to know about that we will extend shortly to support the creation of CareKit activities.

Open Activity.swift. You will see we have defined an activity protocol and the beginnings of our ZCActivity struct which defines an activity . The ZCActivity struct provides an initializer that parses the activity-specific JSON into local immutable properties.

Now open CarePlan.swift. The first thing to note is that the CarePlan struct conforms to the ZCAPIResponse protocol. The initializer will deserialize the JSON file, parse the JSON, and instantiate all the plans properties and activities.

Implementation

Now that you understand the core classes and implementation for loading our Care Plan, let's implement them. Open ViewController.swift and add the following code to the viewdidload() method:

```
let service = newZCService(.Mock)
let mockResource = MockResource(path: "careplan", method: nil, headers: nil,
parameters: nil)
service.request(mockResource) { (response : CarePlan?, error) in
        if error == nil {
            print("\(response!.title) loaded.")
        }
         return
}
```

We start by creating a new service of type .Mock by using our ZCService helper method newZCService. Then create the MockResource specifying the careplan in the path. Recall that *careplan* is the name of our bundled careplan.json file. You can ignore the other parameters as our MockService doesn't use them. Finally we can call the mock service request() method.

Build the project and check that it compiles using Command+B. Then Command+R to run the app in the simulator. If all goes well, you should see the app load after the service request method is called. If it has successfully loaded the Care Plan from the JSON, it will print out in the Debug window the title of the ZombieCare Plan. You may want to play around with this. Try and place a breakpoint in the completion handler and inspect the response in the debugger. You will find it's an instance of CarePlan, and all its properties have been set including an array of ZCActivities.

You will note at this stage we've not used CareKit at all. All we've done is provide a way to load a Care Plan from another resource and map this to some local objects that represent our application business model. Next we will extend these objects to create CareKit activities and load them into the Care Plan Store while providing a more detailed explanation of the CareKit activity, schedule, and event data types.

In this next step we're going to add some support to create CareKit activities. Firstly we'll extend the Activity protocol to specify a createActivity() method and then update ZCActivity to conform to the protocol.

Open Activity.swift from the project navigator. Replace the existing Activity protocol with the following code:

```
protocol Activity {
    var activityType: ActivityType { get set}
    func carePlanActivity() -> OCKCarePlanActivity
}
```

37

Now add the following method to the ZCActivity struct below the initializer:

```
func carePlanActivity() -> OCKCarePlanActivity {

//creates a schedule based on the internal values for start and end dates
let startDateComponents = NSDateComponents(date: self.startDate, calendar:
NSCalendar(calendarIdentifier: NSCalendarIdentifierGregorian)!)

let activitySchedule: OCKCareSchedule!

switch self.scheduleType {
case .Weekly :
    activitySchedule = OCKCareSchedule.weeklyScheduleWithStartDate(startDate
    Components, occurrencesOnEachDay: self.schedule)

case .Daily:
    activitySchedule = OCKCareSchedule.dailyScheduleWithStartDate(startDate
    Components, occurrencesPerDay: self.schedule[0].unsignedIntegerValue)
}

//creates and returns the appropriate CareKit OCKCarePlanActivity
switch activityType {
case .Intervention:
    let activity = OCKCarePlanActivity.interventionWithIdentifier(
        identifier,
        groupIdentifier: nil,
        title: title,
        text: text,
        tintColor: UIColor.greenColor(),
        instructions: instructions,
        imageURL: nil,
        schedule: activitySchedule,
        userInfo: nil)

    return activity
case .Assessment:
    let activity = OCKCarePlanActivity.assessmentWithIdentifier(
        identifier,
        groupIdentifier: nil,
        title: title,
        text: text,
        tintColor: UIColor.greenColor(),
        resultResettable: true,
        schedule: activitySchedule,
        userInfo: nil)

    return activity
    }
}
```

The carePlanActivity() function first creates a CareKit OCKCareSchedule instance using the activities' properties. Note that it uses the Gregorian calendar. It creates an instance of either an intervention or assessment OCKCarePlanActivity, depending on the activity type. The new OCKCarePlanActivity instance is then returned by the function.

Check that the project compiles okay by pressing Command+B.

Let's now take a closer look at the OCKCarePlanActivity and OCKCareSchedule classes in more detail to better understand what they do and how they work.

OCKCarePlanActivity

An instance of the OCKCarePlanActivity class represents a task that the user/patient must complete. Each activity must have a unique identifier, and it has a schedule (OCKCareSchedule) also created by the developer. The schedule determines the number of occurrences of this task for a given day, and each occurrence will be represented by an instance of the OCKPlanEvent, which you'll learn a little more about later.

There are two types of activities defined by the OCKCarePlanActivityType enumeration in CareKit:

- *Intervention activities* are defined by the OCKCarePlanActivityTypeIntervention enum value. These activities are used in the Care Card.

- *Assessment activities* are defined by the OCKCarePlanActivityTypeAssessment enum value. These activities are used by the Symptoms and Measurement Tracker.

As you've seen, developers are responsible for creating activities and their schedules, and we'll see shortly how we can add them to the Care Plan Store using the OCKPlanStore.addActivity() method. But first let's just be clear on the difference between the two types.

Intervention Activities and Events

Intervention activities are for asking the user to do a task related to their treatment. This can be anything you like—for example, taking medication, doing some exercises, or drinking water. These events are displayed in the Care Card.

You'll see later in our example how an intervention activity is presented to the user. For now, all you need to know is that once added to the Care Plan Store, the Care Card ViewController will interact with the Care Plan Store (OCKPlanStore instance) to toggle the state of an activities events. The Activity object will report the completion state of the activity to the Care Plan.

Assessment Activities and Events

Assessment activities are for tracking symptoms and measuring results. They look very similar to intervention activities, but there are two key differences. First, they are resettable. This specifies whether the user is allowed to retake the assessment. Although there is no visual representation of this in the Symptom and Measurement Tracker view, the developer can still decide the behavior if a user wants to redo a completed assessment.

Second, though the intervention activity event just gets its state set to completed or not completed via the Care Card ViewController, with assessment activities the developer is responsible for creating their own custom task or, as mentioned briefly earlier, using ResearchKit tasks.

Once added to the Care Plan Store, the store will lazily generate OCKPlanEvent objects on demand and based on the activity's schedule.

OCKCareSchedule

The OCKCareSchedule specifies the start and end data as well as the recurrence pattern of an activity's schedule. Each activity must have a schedule, and this is based on the Gregorian calendar.

Schedule Types

CareKit provides two predefined schedule types, OCKCareScheduleTypeDaily and OCKCareScheduledTypeWeekly, both of which have supporting initializers in the OCKCareSchedule class implementation. As the names imply, the OCKCareScheduleTypeDaily provides an implementation that returns the number of occurrences of an activity per day, and OCKCareScheduleTypeWeekly provides an implementation that returns the number of occurrences of activity for each day in a week.

There are two classes provided for creating a schedule:

- OCKCareDailySchedule
- OCKCareWeeklySchedule

Each class provides two static class functions to create a schedule.

A Daily Schedule

OCKCareDailySchedule defines a schedule that has the same number of occurrences each day as follows:

```
let startDate = NSDateComponents(year: 2016, month: 01, day: 01)
OCKCareSchedule.dailyScheduleWithStartDate(startDay, occurrencesPerDay: 3)
```

In the preceding example you can see that we create a schedule starting on first day of January 2016. The schedule will create three occurrences of the task per day, or:

```
let startDate = NSDateComponents(year: 2016, month: 01, day: 01)
OCKCareSchedule.dailyScheduleWithStartDate(startDay, occurrencesPerDay: 1,
daysToSkip: 0, endDate: nil)
```

The preceding code is a slight variance on the first method, as it has the additional parameters daysToSkip and endDate. daysToSkip means the number of days between two active days in this period to skip (that is, when no tasks appear). endDate simply means the last day of this schedule. If no endDate is specified, then the schedule is ongoing.

A Weekly Schedule

Alternatively, you might want to create a weekly calendar as follows. OCKCareWeeklySchedule defines a schedule which repeats every week:

```
let startDate = NSDateComponents(year: 2016, month: 01, day: 01)
let schedule = OCKCareSchedule.weeklyScheduleWithStartDate(startDate,
occurrencesOnEachDay: [2, 1, 2, 2, 2, 2, 2])
```

In the preceding example, the schedule again starts on January 1, 2016. But this time we've specified an array of 7 Ints. Each Int maps to a day of the week running from Sunday to Saturday. The value of the Int represents the number of occurrences the task will be scheduled for on its day. In this case, we can see all days have two tasks except Monday, which has one.

Custom Schedules

Developers can also create their own custom schedules.

A third schedule type, OCKCareScheduleTypeOther can be used if you want to subclass the OCKCareSchedule class to support any other type of schedule. For example, you may need a monthly schedule or something more granular like an hourly schedule.

Unfortunately, at the time of writing the CareKit framework has a problem when used with the Swift language (this is not an issue with Objective-C projects) in that you cannot inherit from the OCKCareSchedule class as documented, as the initializer is private. Expect this to be updated in the next point release of the framework. The issues have been acknowledged by the open source development team.

Now that you have a more comprehensive understanding of our activities and their related schedules, we'll complete our implementation in the ZombieCare app and add them to the Care Plan Store.

Adding Activities to the ZombieCare App

First we need to update the CarePlan class so it can retrieve a list of OCKCarePlanActivities by calling the carePlanActivity() method on each ZCActivity we added earlier. Add the following two methods to CarePlan.swift class file after the init() method:

```
func interventionActivities(completion:(activities: [OCKCarePlanActivity])->
Void) {
        let interventionActivities = activities.filter(){$0.activityType ==
        .Intervention}
```

```
    let ckinterventionActivities = interventionActivities.map( {
        $0.carePlanActivity()
    })
    completion(activities: ckinterventionActivities)
}
```

This preceding function first filters and then returns an array of CareKit intervention OCKCarePlanActivity objects by using the filter() and map() and swift functions. The conversion is handled by the carePlanActivity() method we implemented earlier on the ZCActivity class:

```
func assessmentActivities(completion:(activities:
[OCKCarePlanActivity])-> Void) {
    let assessmentActivities = activities.filter(){$0.activityType ==
    .Assessment}
    let ckassessmentActivities = assessmentActivities.map( {
        $0.carePlanActivity()
    })
    completion(activities: ckassessmentActivities)
}
```

As you can see, we do the same for assessment activities. We will actually simplify this later by having a single method to return all CareKit activities, which excludes the filter, but at this stage it seems convenient to be able to retrieve separate lists.

Finally, we need a class that will provide the glue between the CarePlan and ZCActivities we created earlier and for instantiating the CareKit Care Plan Store.

Adding the Care Plan Store Manager

In your ZombieCare project, select the ZombieCare group in the project navigator and then click File ➤ New. Select the iOS Source Swift file and give it the name ZCCarePlanStoreManager. Now copy the following code into the file:

```
import CareKit
class ZCCarePlanStoreManager : NSObject {
    // MARK: Properties
    let store: OCKCarePlanStore
    let carePlan : CarePlan!

    init(carePlan:CarePlan) {
        // Determine the file URL for the store.
        let searchPaths = NSSearchPathForDirectoriesInDomains
        (.ApplicationSupportDirectory, .UserDomainMask, true)
        let applicationSupportPath = searchPaths[0]
        let persistenceDirectoryURL = NSURL(fileURLWithPath:
        applicationSupportPath)
```

```
    if !NSFileManager.defaultManager().fileExistsAtPath(persistenceDirec
    toryURL.absoluteString, isDirectory: nil) {
        try! NSFileManager.defaultManager().createDirectoryAtURL
        (persistenceDirectoryURL, withIntermediateDirectories: true,
        attributes: nil)
    }

    // Create the store.
    store = OCKCarePlanStore(persistenceDirectoryURL:
    persistenceDirectoryURL)
    self.carePlan = carePlan
    super.init()
   }
}
```

The ZCCarePlanStoreManager imports the CareKit framework. It has two key properties: a reference to the OKCarePlanStore and an instance of our CarePlan struct.

Earlier, I described briefly how the Care Plan Store is initialized, and we've now implemented this in the ZCCarePlanStoreManager initializer, providing the directory URL as expected. We also set the carePlan property passed as an instance to the initializer. Now add the following private updateStore() function after the initializer :

```
private func updateStore()-> Void {
    carePlan.interventionActivities { (activities) in
        for activity in activities {
            self.store.addActivity(activity) { success, error in
                                              if !success {
                    print(error?.localizedDescription)
                }
                else {
                    print("Intervention activity \(activity.
                    identifier)  added to careplan store")
                }
            }
        }
    }

    carePlan.assessmentActivities { (activities) in
        for activity in activities {
            self.store.addActivity(activity) { success, error in
                if !success {
                    print(error?.localizedDescription)
                }
```

```
            else {
                print("Assessment activity \(activity.identifier)
                added  to careplan store")
            }
        }
    }
  }
}
```

In this method we retrieve the list of activities that are now converted to our OCKCarePlanActivity objects, and we add each one individually into the Care Plan Store.

Next, call this method in the initializer. Place the following code after the call to super.init() in the classes initializer:

```
self.updateStore()
```

Finally, you need to create am instance of our ZCCarePlanStoreManager. Open the ViewController.swift file and place the following line after the print statement in the service completion handler:

```
_ = ZCCarePlanStoreManager(carePlan: response!)
```

Build and run the project by pressing Command+R. When the application now runs, it loads and parses our ZombieCare Plan. On success it creates an instance of ZCCarePlanStoreManager passing it the Care Plan. In the debugger, you should see some print statements when adding the activities to the CareKit Care Plan Store.

Congratulations! You've now populated your CareKit database. At this stage you might think this is complete, but there's one more thing we need to take care of. You may recall that an activity has a unique identifier field and that you cannot add an activity to the store with the same identifier as one already added. Also we can only actually change the endDate on an activity.

■ **Note**   At the time of writing there is an issue with the addActivity() method in CareKit. The success parameter in the completion handler is not returning the correct response, and therefore it allows us to add an activity even though one exists with the same identifier. When this is corrected in 1.0.1 and you try running the app again, you will find the error is reported. For now, take care how you handle the success value when the method completes.

We will assume that the success code returned in addActivity() will be solved shortly and provide a solution to handle this situation where we want to update an activity. We'll solve the problem by querying the Care Plan Store first, and if an activity exists, we'll remove it and add the new one as we can't update it. We'll also optimize our routine by adding the method to list all activities from our CarePlan.

Add the following method to the CarePlan above the other filter methods:

```
func allActivities(completion:(activities: [OCKCarePlanActivity])-> Void) {
    let ckallActivities = activities.map( {
        $0.carePlanActivity()
    })
    completion(activities: ckallActivities)
}
```

You can see this is bit simpler, as we've removed the filter method, and it should now perform a little faster. Replace the updateStore() method in the ZCCarePlanStoreManager class with this updated version and the new private method to add the activity:

```
private func updateStore()-> Void {
    carePlan.allActivities { (activities) in
        for newactivity in activities {
            self.store.activityForIdentifier(newactivity.identifier,
            completion: { (success, activity, error) in
                if success && activity != nil {
                    self.store.removeActivity(activity!, completion: {
                    (success, error) in
                        if success {
                            self.addActivityToStore(newactivity)
                        }
                    })
                }
                else {
                    self.addActivityToStore(newactivity)
                }
            })
        }
    }
}

private func addActivityToStore(activity: OCKCarePlanActivity) {
    self.store.addActivity(activity) { success, error in
        if !success {
            print(error?.localizedDescription)
        }
        else {
            print("Activity \(activity.identifier) added to careplan
            store")
        }
    }
}
```

We've now handled the scenario where we might be trying to add an existing activity. Be careful, though, when deleting an activity from the store like this—all related events and event results past and present will also be deleted. A better approach might be to set the endDate on the existing activity, leave it in the store, and then add the new activity with a new identifier. You'll want to develop your own strategy on this.

It's worth mentioning at this point that the design of the classes we've used to implement this loading and adding of activities to the Care Plan Store is testable. We've included some tests in the `testTheMockService()` test in the ZombieCareTests target.

To recap on our progress so far, we have now completed the following:

- We defined a ZombieCare Plan that could be stored in JSON format.

- We used a MockService to load the JSON.

- We developed some Care Plan and Activity protocols and classes to model our ZombieCare Plan and activities that are initialized using the JSON data and provide a mechanism to map them to CareKit-specific activities.

- We then added a store manager to coordinate the creation of a CareKit CoreData store and add our activities to it.

The next section discusses how to query the Care Plan Store for activities, events, and event results and how to subscribe to the Care Plan Store delegate to receive updates on changes to the store. To begin, we need to understand two more data types: OCKCarePlanEvent and OCKCarePlanEventResult.

OCKCarePlanEvent

An instance of OCKCarePlanEvent is an occurrence of an event. As demonstrated earlier, an activity has a schedule, and each schedule has an array of occurrences plus a method that returns the number of events on a given date.

Each event has two unique indices that define it:

- *numberOfDaysSinceStart*: This indicates the number or index of this event since the start date. For example, if the event is on the second day, its index would be 1.

- *occurrenceIndexOfDay*: This is the index of the event on a given day, because we can have an activity that has multiple events in day. For example, if an event has three occurrences in a day, then it would be represented by three OCKCarePlanEvent instances with indices from 0,1,2.

Other properties include the following:

- *date*: The date that this event occurs.

- *activity*: A reference to its related parent activity.

- *state*: An OCKCarePlanEventState can have one of three states: Initialized, NotComplete, and Completed.

- *result*: A reference to an OCKCarePlanEventResult.

The good news is that we do not have to create OCKCarePlanEvents. This is all handled by the OCKPlanStore when an activity is referenced via its API. But you can query the store for events and get notified of updates to events by subscribing to the OCKCarePlanStoreDelegate, and you can update the state of an event. The OCKPlanStore provides an API for these procedures.

OCKCarePlanEventResult

The OCKCarePlanEventResult class provides us with an instance of a result for the OCKPlanEvent. You can create an instance of a result and attach it to an an event using the OCKPlanStore API. OCKCarePlanEventResult will be used to create results for assessment activity events only.

There are three properties of OCKCarePlanEventResult:

- *creationDate*: The time the result was created

- *valueString*: A string representation of the result value

- *unitString*: A string representation of the result unit

In addition to the simple result type, OCKCarePlanEventResult extends HealthKit. This can be useful when creating a result that can be related to a Healthkit sample, category, or correlation type—for example, a weight measurement. It makes sense to store this value in Healthkit when we record it so it can be used by other applications, which lets us avoid saving duplicate data.

In this case you initialize the OCKCarePlanEventResult instance with the HealthKit sample and then add this to the store. The store only saves the sample UUID and formatting parameters and thus it enables it to fetch the actual HealthKit sample when required. In later chapters we'll work through an example of this.

Reading Data from the Store

CareKit's Care Card ViewController and the Symptom and Measurement Tracker ViewController are both used to display all the events for the intervention and assessment activities, respectively. You can build an app that uses these modules and never have to actually query the Care Plan Store for activities at all. However, it might prove to be useful and even prudent to do so.

We've already seen when working with a Care Plan that we can load from a remote resource, and that we need to be careful about how we add and update activities, because it will not accept duplicates. Chapter 1 also outlined the method for querying for activities. This section gives examples of additional methods provided on the OCKPlanStore API.

47

This is the query we used earlier to check whether an activity with the same identifier already existed in the Care Plan Store. You implemented this in the previous section:

```
store.activityForIdentifier("ActivityID") { (success, activity, error) in
        guard success else {
                        error!.localizedDescription
                }
            //Do something with the activity
    }
```

This query finds all actives with the same group identifier—it could be useful when you want to logically group activities:

```
store.activitiesWithGroupIdentifier("OurCustomGroup") { (success, activities,
error) in
                guard success else {
                  error!.localizedDescription
            }
        //Do something with the activities

}
```

This query fetches actives for a specific type, such as .Intervention or .Assessment:

```
store.activitiesWithType(.Intervention) { (success, activities, error) in
            guard success else {
                  error!.localizedDescription
        }
        //Do something with the activities
}
```

The following fetches all activities:

```
store.activitiesWithCompletion { (success, activities, error) in
            guard success else {
                  error!.localizedDescription
        }
        //Do something with the activities

}
```

You can determine your own requirements to see if you need to call any of the queries. For ZombieCare we'll stick with the activityForIdentifier query as demonstrated.

There are no limitations to the number of events that an activity can have, so we need to be careful about how we query the Care Plan Store—otherwise we could end up with a very large memory footprint in the app. CareKit therefore provides APIs that only allow us to query for events for a single day.

The following is an example of a query that reads all intervention events for the Ibuprofen activity for today:

```
guard let calendar = NSCalendar(calendarIdentifier:
NSCalendarIdentifierGregorian) else {
    fatalError("This should never fail.")
}

let today = calendar.components([.Day, .Month, .Year], fromDate: NSDate())
store.eventsForActivity(ibuprofenActivity, date: today) { (events,
errorOrNil) in

    guard success else {
        fatalError(error!.localizedDescription)
    }

    // do something with the events.
}
```

First we create a Gregorian calendar and set its components for day, months, and year for today. Then call eventsForActivity() passing the ibuprofenActivity activity and the NSDateComponent object. In the completion handler, you receive all events for the activity for that date or an error. Note here that CareKit uses the NSDateComponent object so that we can specify a unique date from the user's perspective, regardless of their time zone.

Additional CareKit Methods

There are two additional higher order methods that CareKit provides to help you iterate over a larger numbers of events:

```
store.dailyCompletionStatusWithType(ibuprofenActivity, startDate: startDate,
endDate: endDate, handler: { (date, completed, total) in
        // This block is called once for each date.
        let percentComplete = Double(completed) / Double(total)
        completionData.append((dateComponents, percentComplete))
        }) { (success, error) in
            // This block is called after the last date's handler
            returns.
                guard success else {
                    fatalError(error!.localizedDescription)
                }

    }
```

This first method gets the number of completed events for each day. Let's look at the method more closely. The first parameter passed is the activity we want to find events for. We specify the date range using startDate and endDate.

The first completion handler returns a date, the number of completed events on that day, and the total events on that day. This handler is called for each date in the date range. The second completion handler is called after the last date handler returns.

The dailyCompletionStatusWithType method is useful if, for example, you want to display the percent status for each individual day. In fact, the Care Card and Symptom and Measurement Tracker ViewControllers both use this to update their weekly view and overall heart indicators.

In the next function, we can query for all the events of an activity within a given date range:

```
store.enumerateEventsOfActivity(ibuprofenActivity, startDate: startdate,
endDate: endDate, handler: { (event, stop) in
        // This block is called once for each event
        if let event = eventOrNil,
            result = event.result,
            value = Double(result.valueString) {
    }
    }) { (success, error) in
        // This block is called after the last event's handler returns.
        guard success else {
            // Add proper error handling here...
            fatalError(error!.localizedDescription)
        }
    }
```

This second function also passes the activity and date range as parameters to the function.

The first completion handler is called for each event and passes the event and second parameter that we've called stop. stop is the address of a bool, and you can set this to true in your handler to break out of the enumeration. The second completion handler is called after the last event has been returned.

The enumerateEventsOfActivity method is useful for fetching a list of events—for example, if we want to query all the events and generate some insights.

Synchronizing the Functions

Note that both functions are asynchronous. It's possible that you may need to synchronize your calls to these functions. One option is to use GCD. Using GCD you can surround your calls using a couple of different approaches.

One approach might be to use a semaphore. This would look similar to this:

```
let semaphore = dispatch_semaphore_create(0)
// Call the function and process handler
```

```
// Use the semaphore to signal that the query is complete in the completion
handler.
dispatch_semaphore_signal(semaphore)
// After the function call wait for the semaphore to be signalled.
dispatch_semaphore_wait(semaphore, DISPATCH_TIME_FOREVER)
```

Another approach might be to use GCD despatch groups. This is useful if you want to call both asynchronous events one after the other and then collate the results once both have completed.

■ **Note** If you're not familiar with GCD, you can find more information in Apple's documentation.

Other alternative functions for retrieving events from the Care Plan Store include the following:

```
store.eventsOnDate(date, type: .Intervention) { (eventsGroupedByActivity,
error) in
        //
        }
```

The preceding gets all the OCKCarePlanEvent objects for a given date. Note that events are grouped by activity:

```
store.eventsForActivity(activity, date: date) { (events, error) in
        //
        }
```

The preceding gets events on a given date that belong to a OCKCarePlanActivity.

You've now seen how to query the Care Plan Store for events and when you might want to use the different methods. In the next few chapters we'll apply one or more of these functions in the ZombieCare app. But first you will learn how to get notified when changes are made to the Care Plan Store and how we can use this in our ZombieCare app to to update the app.

OCKCarePlanStoreDelegate

CareKit provides us with the OCKCarePlanStoreDelegate delegate. You can implement this delegate to subscribe to changes in the store.

didReceiveUpdateOfEvent() is used to get notified when an activity event is updated, and carePlanStoreActivityListDidChange() is called when an activity is added or removed from the store.

Our ZombieCare app needs to respond to these events for two reasons:

- We need to update the Insights view dashboard if there are changes to events.

- If we have a custom Care Card or Symptom and Measurement Tracker view, then we need to handle updates from the Care Plan Store after events have been updated.

Whereas the Care Card ViewController registers and handles both the preceding events, the Symptom and Measurement Tracker ViewController registers for and handles the events update method only. The Insights ViewController does neither. The reason for this is that the Insights dashboard has no direct relation or use for activities or events. Instead it relies only on insight items. An insight to the patient's condition is something that might be created from a number of different sources, not just activity events.

Let's extend our ZCCarePlanStoreManager to subscribe to the OCKCarePlanStoreDelegate activity and event changes. This will enable us to get notified of the Care Plan Store changes, which we can notify other objects about if required.

Open the ZCCarePlanStoreManager.swift file. At the bottom of the file, add the following extension:

```swift
extension ZCCarePlanStoreManager: OCKCarePlanStoreDelegate {
    func carePlanStoreActivityListDidChange(store: OCKCarePlanStore) {
        print("Care Plan Store Activity list updated")
    }

    func carePlanStore(store: OCKCarePlanStore, didReceiveUpdateOfEvent
    event: OCKCarePlanEvent) {
        print("Care Plan Store event updated")
    }
}
```

Now register the ZCCarePlanStoreManager object as the delegate so it gets notified of changes by adding the following code below the call to `super.init()` in the initializer:

```swift
store.delegate = self
```

Press Command+R to build and run the app in the simulator. You should now see the message "Care Plan Store Activity list updated" printed out in the Debug window, which indicates to us that the ZCCarePlanStoreManager object has received notifications when activities are added to the store.

Notice that we are not seeing any messages about event updates. The reason for this is that events are not created until the Care Plan Store is queried. This would usually happen when the Care Card ViewController or Symptom and Measurement ViewController views are opened.

Let's now extend ZCCarePlanStoreManager with its own new delegate that other objects can register to if they need updates. We're going to be fairly specific here and have a delegate that will notify observers of changes when there are updated insights only.

Add the following delegate protocol to the bottom of the ZCCarePlanStoreManager. swift file:

```
protocol ZCCarePlanStoreManagerDelegate: class {
    func zcCarePlanStoreManager(manager: ZCCarePlanStoreManager,
    didUpdateInsights insights: [OCKInsightItem])
}
```

This protocol defines the didUpdateInsights method, which includes a list of CareKit OCKInsightItems.

Add the following property above the declaration of the Care Plan Store property:

```
weak var delegate: ZCCarePlanStoreManagerDelegate?
```

We've now prepared the ZCCarePlanStoreManager to respond to updates when activities or events are changed, added, or removed, and we've added a mechanism for us to notify other objects if and when we create any insights as a result of the changes.

Clearing the Store

Before closing this chapter, there is one more item to address. In some cases , particularly when testing, it might be useful to clear the store of all items. Apple provides a method to demonstrate how to do this, and it looks like this:

```
private func _clearStore() {
    print("*** CLEANING STORE DEBUG ONLY ****")
    let deleteGroup = dispatch_group_create()
    let store = self.store
    dispatch_group_enter(deleteGroup)
    store.activitiesWithCompletion { (success, activities, errorOrNil) in
        guard success else {
            // Perform proper error handling here...
            fatalError(errorOrNil!.localizedDescription)
        }
        for activity in activities {
            dispatch_group_enter(deleteGroup)
            store.removeActivity(activity) { (success, error) -> Void in
                print("Removing \(activity)")
                guard success else {
                    fatalError("*** An error occurred: \(error!.
                    localizedDescription)")
                }
                print("Removed: \(activity)")
                dispatch_group_leave(deleteGroup)
            }
        }
```

```
        dispatch_group_leave(deleteGroup)
    }
    // Wait until all the asynchronous calls are done.
    dispatch_group_wait(deleteGroup, DISPATCH_TIME_FOREVER)
}
```

Summary

This chapter has covered a lot. We've learned what the Care Plan Store is and how to create it. We've added, updated, and removed activities and we've seen how to query the store in different ways for activities and events. We've also seen how to get notified of changes in the store. We also extended our working example in the ZombieCare app to load a Care Plan from JSON, parse it, load its data into the store, and then receive notifications when activities or events are updated. Finally, we provided a mechanism for other objects in our app to get notified by ZCCarePlanStoreManager when insights are created or updated.

The next chapter covers the Care Card ViewController in more detail. You will learn how to create and display the Care Card ViewController, see how it gets updated, and customize its appearance. You will then add a custom Care Card Detail ViewController.

CHAPTER 4

∎ ∎ ∎

Building the Care Card

Chapter 1 gave you an introduction to the Care Card ViewController, and Chapter 3 talked about the underlying data model and types used by the Care Plan and, ultimately, the CareKit views. In this chapter we'll take a closer look at the Care Card ViewController user interface, learn how to create one and display it, and then customize it. We'll do this by extending our ZombieCare app.

The user interface for the ZombieCare app is deliberately going to remain simple, starting out as a single view application. The template provided is in the folder \chapter4_ start and begins where we left off in chapter3_final with a few additions. Load the project and run it in the simulator now.

You will see that we've added a new introductory view to the ZombieCare Plan called CarePlanViewController.swift. This will be our initial ViewController in the application, and its purposes are to introduce the user to the ZombieCare Plan and provide an entry point to the Care Plan itself. You may want to design a different user experience, but this serves our purpose well and allows us to add some additional onboarding in later chapters.

In addition to the CarePlanViewController, you'll see we've added an additional TabBarController into the storyboard. The TabBarController will host our CareKit modules, and there will be an entry point to load the TabBarController from CarePlanViewController.swift.

Building and Presenting a Care Card

Open CarePlanViewController.swift from the project navigator.

In viewDidLoad() replace the call to the existing service.request method with the following:

```
service.request(mockResource) { (response : CarePlan?, error) in
        if error == nil {
            print("\(response!.title) loaded.")
            self.careplanManager = ZCCarePlanStoreManager(carePlan:
            response!)
```

```
            self.carePlanTitle.text = self.careplanManager?.carePlan.
            title
            self.carePlanDescription.text = self.careplanManager?.
            carePlan.carePlanDescription
        }
        return
    }
```

This now reads the title and description from the Care Plan and displays the text in the view.

Next, add the following createCareCardViewController() method to the bottom of the class:

```
private func createCareCardViewController() -> OCKCareCardViewController {
        let viewController = OCKCareCardViewController(carePlanStore:
        careplanManager!.store)

        // Setup the controller's title and tab bar item
        viewController.title = NSLocalizedString("Zombie Care Card",
        comment: "")
        viewController.tabBarItem = UITabBarItem(title: viewController.
        title, image: UIImage(named:"carecard"), selectedImage:
        UIImage(named: "carecard-filled"))

        return viewController
    }
```

First, this creates an instance of the OCKCareCardViewController, passing to it the Care Plan Store object.

The ViewControllers title is localized, and then we added a UITabBarItem, which consists of the tab title and its image.

In the BuildCareCard() button handler, add the following:

```
let storyboard = UIStoryboard(name: "Main", bundle: nil)
let tabbarcontroller = storyboard.instantiateViewControllerWithIdentifier
("TabBarController") as! UITabBarController
let careCardViewController = createCareCardViewController()
tabbarcontroller.viewControllers = [UINavigationController(rootViewControll
er: careCardViewController)]

self.presentViewController(tabbarcontroller, animated: true, completion: nil)
```

In the preceding code, we first load the TabBarController from the main storyboard using its Storyboard ID. We then make a call to createCarCardController() to build the Care Card ViewController, which is then attached to the TabBars array of ViewControllers.

■ **Note**   The Care Card ViewController must be embedded in a UINavigationController—
otherwise, CareKit will Assert. This is because Care Card uses a navigation controller to push
and display the Care Card detail view.

In the last line we present the tab bar, which loads and displays the Care Card.
Press Command+R to build and run the app in the simulator. You should be
presented with the CarePlanViewController, which has a button to "Begin Your
Treatment." Tap the button, and your CareKit Tab should be loaded with the Card Card
presented as the one and only tab. The Care Card should look like Figure 4-1.

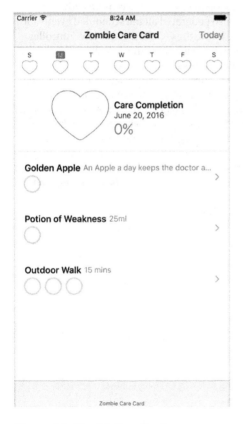

Figure 4-1. *Zombie Care Card*

A Closer Look at the Care Card

Let's examine the Card Card a little closer. At the top of the Care Card, the localized title we set earlier is displayed in the navigation bar. Underneath this is the week view, which defaults to Today. In the week view, a heart image is displayed for each day of the week. Each one of these hearts is color filled with the percentage of tasks complete for their respective days.

Below this is a larger heart for the current day. Again this indicates the percentage of tasks completed for the displayed day. You can try selecting different days and then toggle tasks to on and off to see the varying results.

Below the week view we have a list of intervention activities presented in a table view. Each row displays the activities' title and summary property. Within each activity there are a number of events, each represented by a circular image button.

You should also see that the Care Card has loaded all the .Intervention activities automatically from the Care Plan Store. It has also generated all the scheduled events for each activity as green circle buttons. Under the hood, the OCKCareCardViewController has made a call to the OCKPlanStore instance to fetch all the events by calling eventsOnDate(), which returns a list of OCKPlanEvents grouped by activity.

There are a few more items to take notice of. The OCKCareCardViewController only supports up to 14 events for each activity. You will need to test and ensure that your schedule does not exceed this—otherwise, an exception will be thrown. Any changes you make will be automatically saved by the Care Plan. For instance when toggling the state of an event. Only activities with the OCKCarePlanActivityType .Intervention type are displayed in the Care Card.

Each activity row has a disclosure button. Selecting a row will present the OCKCareCardDetailsViewController, which displays additional details for the selected activity—for instance, the instructions.

Figure 4-2 shows the default Care Card details view.

Figure 4-2. *Default Care Card detail view*

At this point it would be a good idea to try and experiment a bit. Try modifying your Care Plan with additional activities and then re-run the app to see the effects.

Updating the Care Card

As mentioned in the previous section, the Care Card is automatically updated when changes are made to the Care Plan Store. Let's take a moment to understand how this works. This will prove useful if you're considering presenting your own custom view of the Care Plan.

The approach taken in OCKCareCardViewController is to first subscribe to changes from the Care Plan store by implementing the OCKPlanStoreDelegate.

carePlanStoreActivityListDidChange() is called when an activity is added or removed from the store. In this case, the OCKCareCardViewController calls its own fetchEvents() method (described in the next section).

`didReceiveUpdateOfEvent()` is called when one of the events in the Care Plan Store is updated. In this case, the controller finds the related activity, and if the UI is displaying an event for the same day as the modified event, it updates the UI.

The `fetchEvents()` method on the controller is also called when the view is first loaded—or more specifically, when a particular week day is selected. This method will query the Care Plan Store using the API method `eventsOnDate()`. On completion, the context is switched to the main thread, and the list of events returned in the query is copied to a local mutable array before updating the UI.

Customizing the Behavior of OCKCareCardViewController

In addition to handling the OCKPlanStoreDelegate, you can also handle events on OCKCareCardViewControllerDelegate to customize some of its behavior—for example, if you wanted the user to perform some activity to complete an event.

One delegate we can handle is the `shouldHandleEventCompletionForActivity()`, which works in combination with the `didSelectButtonWithInterventionEvent()` event. You can choose this to handle these delegate events if you want to customize the behavior when setting the state of an event—for example, if you want the user to complete an additional task, or ask them a question.

To demonstrate this, we'll extend the ZombieCare app to prompt the user to confirm that they want to change an events state.

The first step to handling the delegate is to refactor our application slightly so we can write an extension delegate which handles the OCKCareCardViewControllerDelegate methods. Open the project and add a new file called ZCCarePlanTabViewController.swift. Add the following class implementation:

```
import UIKit
import CareKit

class ZCCarePlanTabViewController : UITabBarController {
    var careplanManager : ZCCarePlanStoreManager?
}
```

We declare the class and add a property for our ZCCarePlanStoreManager, which we'll need to access to get to the Care Plan Store.

Now open the Main.storyboard in interface builder. Select the TabViewController and change it to use the our new custom class ZCCarePlanTabViewController in the attributes inspector, as in Figure 4-3.

Figure 4-3. *Changing TabbarController class*

Now open CarePlanViewController.swift and in the `BuildCareCard()` method change the implementation so it loads our custom tab bar class as follows:

```
let tabbarcontroller = storyboard.instantiateViewControllerWithIdentifier
("TabBarController") as! ZCCarePlanTabViewController
```

Below this add the following line to set the property of the CarePlanStoreManager:

```
tabbarcontroller.careplanManager = self.careplanManager
```

By injecting our Care Plan Store manager into the ZCCarePlanTabViewController property, it is still testable and allows the controller delegate to access the CareKit store.

We can now implement OCKCareCardViewControllerDelegate. Open the ZCCarePlanTabViewController.swift file and add the following extension code to the bottom of the file:

```
extension ZCCarePlanTabViewController : OCKCareCardViewControllerDelegate {

    func careCardViewController(viewController: OCKCareCardViewController,
    shouldHandleEventCompletionForActivity interventionActivity:
    OCKCarePlanActivity) -> Bool {
        return false;
    }

    func careCardViewController(viewController: OCKCareCardViewController,
    didSelectButtonWithInterventionEvent interventionEvent:
    OCKCarePlanEvent) {

        let alert = UIAlertController(title: "Confirmation", message: "Are
        you sure you want to mark this event as done?", preferredStyle:
        UIAlertControllerStyle.Alert) alert.addAction(UIAlertAction
        (title: "No", style: UIAlertActionStyle.Default, handler: nil))
```

```
    alert.addAction(UIAlertAction(title: "Yes", style:
    UIAlertActionStyle.Default, handler: { (alert) in
        self.careplanManager?.store.updateEvent(interventionEvent,
        withResult: nil, state: .Completed, completion: { (success,
        event, error) in
            print("Yes confirmed - Event updated")
        })
    }))

    self.presentViewController(alert, animated: true, completion: nil)
    }
}
```

We first handle the 'shouldHandleEventCompletionForActivity()' event and return false. This tells the Card Card ViewController that we have some custom logic we want to implement for the completion activity.

We then handle the `didSelectButtonWithInterventionEvent()`, event which is called when the user taps on an intervention event button. Now this is where we can implement our own custom behavior to complete the event. In our example we simply present an AlertView to ask the user to confirm that they want to change the events status. You could quite easily present your own custom ViewController to the user with another task or questionnaire at this point.

On confirmation, the event status is changed to .Complete by calling the `updateEvent()` method on the Care Plan Store.

▓ **Note**   You cannot just change the properties of an event directly yourself. This has to be handled via the Care Plan Store API.

Another event, the `willDisplayEvents()` delegate method, is called from within the OCKCareCardViewControllers `fetchEvents()` method, that is, after it loads all events from the Care Plan Store.

▓ **Note**   Be careful because the documentation is not entirely accurate here. It says that this event is called when an event date changes or when the carePlanStoreActivityListDidChange delegate method is called.

Handling this method can be useful because it provides an opportunity to update the store. For example, you may want to get updated data from HealthKit or elsewhere. We've not implemented this.

In the following section we will implement the `didSelectRowWithInterventionActivity()` event to enable us to present our own Care Card Detail ViewController.

Customizing the Care Card Appearance

The default appearance of the Care Card can be modified in a number of ways:

- Change activity colors

- Display or hide the activity row edge indicators.

- Change the mask images and tint color (for example, replace the heart with something else)

- Provide a custom Care Card details view

We'll learn how to accomplish all of these in the next steps with our ZombieCare app.

Changing Activity Event Colors

You can change the color of the event display buttons for an activity, and each activity can have a different color.

The OCKCarePlanActivity class has a tintColor property. When the event for an activity is loaded and displayed in a TableViewCell, this property is referenced to set the color of the event buttons in the cell.

Lets see this in action. We're going to update our Care Plan to give each intervention activity a different color and see this reflected automatically in the view. To achieve this, we will update the activities in careplan.json with an additional color property as a string. We've also provided a UIColor extension that can convert the color string values to a UIColor.

Go ahead and modify your careplan.json to include the following color attributes:

```
"intervention_activities": [
                                {
                                ...
                                "color": "Gold",
                                ...
                                },
                                {
                                ...
                                "color": "Purple",
                                ...
                                },
                                {
                                ...
                                "color": "Orange",
                                ...
                                }
                                ],
```

```
"assessment_activities": [
                        {
                        ...
                        "color": "Gold",
                        ...
                        },
                        {
                        ...
                        "color": "Purple",
                          ....
                        },
                        {
                        ...
                          "color": "Orange",
                        ...
                        }
                        ]
```

Now you will update the ZCActivity struct to support loading and parsing the colors. Add the optional color property to ZCActivity:

```
let colorcolorcolor : UIColor?
```

Add the following to initialize the color from the JSON source in the initializer:

```
let colorcolorcolorString = json["colorcolorcolor"].string!
self.colorcolorcolor = UIColor.ColorWithString(colorcolorString)
```

Now in the carePlanActivity() method, modify the OCKCarePlanActivity initializers with the color as follows:

```
switch activityType {
        case .Intervention:
            let activity = OCKCarePlanActivity.interventionWithIdentifier(
                identifier,
                groupIdentifier: nil,
                title: title,
                text: text,
                tintColor: color,
                instructions: instructions,
                imageURL: nil,
                schedule: activitySchedule,
                userInfo: nil)
```

```
            return activity
    case .Assessment:
        let activity = OCKCarePlanActivity.assessmentWithIdentifier(
            identifier,
            groupIdentifier: nil,
            title: title,
            text: text,
            tintColor: color,
            resultResettable: true,
            schedule: activitySchedule,
            userInfo: nil)

        return activity
    }
```

■ **Note**   Our ZombieCare app currently only supports the three colors: gold, purple, and orange. You can look to create your own solution for parsing colors depending on your requirement.

You can now run the app in the simulator by pressing Command+R. When you display the Care Card, it should now show the events in their own colors.

Hide/Display Event Row Indicators

Event row indicators are a color strip on the left edge of each row in the list of activities. You can toggle the display of this strip of color by simply turning on or off the showEdgeIndicators property on the OCKCareCardViewController.

Let's turn these on. In our CarePlanViewController.swift file, scroll down to the createCardViewController() method. Add the following code below the line which creates the UITabBarItem:

```
viewController.showEdgeIndicators = true
```

Run the app and you will see the strips being displayed in the same color as the round buttons.

Changing the Mask Tint Color and Mask Images

Changing the mask tint color is straightforward. Simply set the maskImageTintColor property when creating the CareCardViewController:

```
viewController.maskImageTintColorColorColor = UIColor.
MaskTintColorColorColor()
```

We do this in the `CarePlanViewController.createCareCardViewController()` method. Note the `MaskTintColor()` is implemented in our extension on UIColor.

We can further customize the Care Card interface by changing the heart images in the WeekView to our own custom images.

There are two image properties we can set on the OCKCareCardViewController:

- *smallMaskImage*: This is the image that will be used to fill in the week days at the top of the week view. You should provide three sizes: @3x is 94 x 80, @2x is 62 x 52, and @1x is 31 x 26.

- *maskImage*: This is the image that will be used to fill in the percentage complete for the week. You should provide three sizes: @3x is 352 x 296, @2x is 234 x 197, and @1x is 118 x 99.

For both images you should provide a .png that has an outline that is best matched to your tint color, a white fill, and a transparent background.

In our ZombieCare app, I've already provided you with a collection of image masks (Figure 4-4) called brain and small-brain in the Assets catalog of Chapter4_final. (It seemed appropriate given that the Zombie virus affects the brain.)

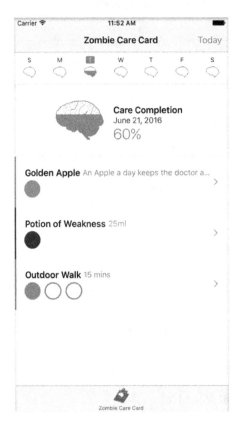

Figure 4-4. *Custom image masks*

Changing the Tab Icon

You may notice in Figure 4-4 that we've also added a custom tab bar icon.

TabBar icons should be included in the Assets catalog. You will find two images in chapter4_final: one for normal state and one for the selected state. For each image, you should provide three sizes: @3x is 90 x 90, @2x is 60 x 60, and @1x is 30 x 30.

You tell the Care Card to use your specific icons when creating the tabbaritem, which we did earlier in the `CarePlanViewController.createCareCardViewController()` method:

```
viewController.tabBarItem = UITabBarItem(title: viewController.title, image:
UIImage(named:"carecard"), selectedImage: UIImage(named: "carecard-filled"))
```

Custom Care Card Detail View

There are a couple of approaches to customizing the Care Card detail view:

- You can add an image to the default detail view.

- You can replace the default OCKCareCardDetailViewController with a custom controller and view.

Adding an Image to the Intervention Activity

The OCKCarePlanActivity class has an optional property to specify an imageURL. As an NSURL, your image could be served from a remote server or simply bundled as a resource within the application.

This can be very useful—for instance, if you need to provide some visual instructions to help the patient take their treatment.

To demonstrate this feature, you will include an image resource in careplan.json. However, for convenience we will bundle the resources in the application. Our image will show a zombie how to eat an apple, as they might be in a bit of a confused state and may have forgotten how to do it.

■ **Note**   Because we cannot specify an NSURL path to our Assets catalog, our image is bundled as a standard resource file in the project.

Open careplan.json and add the image attribute for the first intervention activity as follows:

```
"imageURL": "zombie.jpg",
```

Now open the Activity.swift file and you will modify the initialiser to load the imageurl as follows:

```
if let imageString = json["imageURL"].string {
        let componentsOfString = imageString.
        componentsSeparatedByString(".")
```

```
    if let pathForResource = NSBundle.mainBundle().pathForResource
    (componentsOfString[0], ofType: componentsOfString[1]){
        self.imageURL = NSURL(fileURLWithPath: pathForResource)
    }
}
```

Thats all there is to it, as you've already specified the imageURL property on the OCKPlanActivity initializer.

Press Command+R to run in the simulator, navigate to the Care Card detail view for the intervention activity you added the image to, and you should see your zombie image, as in Figure 4-5.

Figure 4-5. *Images with the Care Card detail view*

Writing Your Own Custom Care Card Detail View

The second approach to customizing the Care Card detail view is to substitute the default controller with your own custom implementation.

In this section you will learn how to do this by creating a new ViewController that displays information with a different layout and also uses the additional activity property userinfo for some custom data properties. This enables us to add and save some custom data with the OCKCarePlanActivity that can also be used or displayed in our new detail view. Here are the steps we need to achieve our goal:

1. Add some custom data to the care plan.

2. Provide support in the ZCActivity to parse, save, and retrieve the custom data.

3. Create the custom detail view and controller implementation.

4. Implement careCardViewController.didSelectRowWith InterventionActivity() to load and display the custom detail view.

For the first step you are going to add some additional information about the treatment medication and also an image of it to the Care Plan. This should help the zombies.

Add the following to each of the intervention activities after the instructions field:

```
"intervention_activities": [
                            {
                            ...
                            "medication" : "There are two types of
                            golden apple.  You need to find and eat a
                            golden apple that is glowing. If its not
                            glowing then it won't work.",
                            "medicationimage" : "glowingapple.png"
                            },
                            {
                            ...
                            "medication" : "Potion of weakness is
                            generally applied by your physician who will
                            splash it on you,  but you can drink it as
                            well.",
                            "medicationimage" : "potionweakness.png"
                            },
                            {
                            ...
                            "medication" : "This assumes you are in a
                            condition to walk. If you can't, just move
                            any part of your body repeatably - like
                            nodding your head.",
                            "medicationimage" : "zombiepressup.png"
                            }
                            ],
```

■ **Note** If you're not sure how to add this, you can always look at the source code from the chapter4_final folder.

Next, you need to load, parse, and include the new custom data to the OCKPlanActivities. To do this, you need to provide a custom object that supports NSCoding.

From the project navigator in the ZombieCare project, select New File. Select Swift File and call it Medication.

Now copy the following into the file:

```swift
import Foundation

class Medication : NSObject,  NSCoding {
    let medication : String
    let imageURL : NSURL

    init?(medication : String, imageURL : NSURL ) {
        self.medication = medication
        self.imageURL = imageURL
    }

    // MARK: NSCoding
    required convenience init?(coder decoder: NSCoder) {

        let medication = decoder.decodeObjectForKey("medication") as! String
        let imageURL = decoder.decodeObjectForKey("imageURL")as! NSURL

        self.init(medication:medication, imageURL: imageURL)
    }

    func encodeWithCoder(coder: NSCoder) {
        coder.encodeObject(self.medication, forKey: "medication")
        coder.encodeObject(self.imageURL, forKey: "imageURL")

    }
}
```

Import the Foundation framework, because it needs this to provide support for NSObject and NSCoding.

In the class implementation you have two properties: one for the medication string and the other for an image URL. Then it provides a custom initialiser and support for NSCoding. This class is now ready to represent the new custom medication fields.

You then need to update the ZCActivity struct so it can use the Medication class. Add the following property below the existing properties:

```swift
var medication : Medication? = nil
```

And add the following code to the end of the init method:

```
if let medication = json["medication"].string,
         let medicationImageString = json["medicationimage"].string {
         let componentsOfString = medicationImageString.
         componentsSeparatedByString(".")
         let pathForResource = NSBundle.mainBundle().pathForResource
         (componentsOfString[0],  ofType: componentsOfString[1])

         self.medication = Medication(medication: medication, imageURL:
         NSURL(fileURLWithPath: pathForResource!))
    }
```

This first line parses the medication properties from the JSON and then instantiates a Medication object using the parsed values before assigning it to the property.

The last task for this step is to add this Medication object to our OCKCarePlanActivity when it is created. In the carePlanActivity() method add the following just before the switch activityType statement:

```
var medicationDict : [String : Medication]? = nil

if let meds = medication {
    medicationDict = ["medication":meds]
}
```

This creates an optional dictionary.

Now in the switch statement set the userinfo parameter in the intervention initializer from nil to the following:

```
userInfo: medicationDict)
```

userInfo takes a dictionary of objects that support NSCoding. You can add more than one object if you like.

Thats it for the second step. Press Command+B to check that the project still compiles okay.

The third step is to create the custom detail ViewController to replace the default OCKCareCardDetailViewController. Select File ➤ New from the project navigator again. This time select Cocoa Touch Class from the iOS section. Give it the name ZCCareCardDetailViewController and ensure its a subclass of UIViewController. Select Next and then Create. You now have the basic template of the new class.

In this new class you need to provide a custom initializer, a property to hold our OCKPlanActivity, and some custom layout. Let's start with the property. Add the following line to set the intervention property at the top of the class:

```
let interventionActivity : OCKCarePlanActivity?
```

And then add the following initializers:

```
init(withInterventionActivity:OCKCarePlanActivity) {
    self.interventionActivity = withInterventionActivity
    super.init(nibName: nil, bundle: nil)
}

required init?(coder aDecoder: NSCoder) {
    self.interventionActivity = nil
    super.init(coder: aDecoder)
}
```

You've added a custom initializer with a parameter for the OCKPlanActivity, and, because we inherit from UIViewController, you are required to provide an additional init with coder initializer. In the case of the latter, you are just setting the property to nil as you won't be using this initializer in the project.

Because this is just a demonstration for learning, we're going to keep the UI simple and just implement the medication properties. Add the following code to the class:

```
override func viewWillAppear(animated: Bool) {
    super.viewWillAppear(animated)

    self.view.backgroundColor = UIColor.whiteColor()

    if let medication = self.interventionActivity?.
    userInfo!["medication"] as? Medication {

        let label = UILabel()
        label.numberOfLines = 0
        label.lineBreakMode = .ByWordWrapping
        label.textAlignment = .Center
        label.translatesAutoresizingMaskIntoConstraints = false
        label.text = medication.medication
        self.view.addSubview(label)
        view.addConstraints([
            NSLayoutConstraint(item: label, attribute: .Top, relatedBy:
            .Equal, toItem: view, attribute: .Top, multiplier: 1.0,
            constant: 120.0),
            NSLayoutConstraint(item: label, attribute: .Leading,
            relatedBy: .Equal, toItem: view, attribute: .Leading,
            multiplier: 1.0, constant: 20.0),
            NSLayoutConstraint(item: label, attribute: .Trailing,
            relatedBy: .Equal, toItem: view, attribute: .Trailing,
            multiplier: 1.0, constant: -20.0)
            ])
```

```
        if let image = UIImage(contentsOfFile: medication.imageURL.
        path!) {

            let imageView = UIImageView(image: image)
            imageView.translatesAutoresizingMaskIntoConstraints = false

            self.view.addSubview(imageView)
    //Manually add some constraints
            view.addConstraints([
                NSLayoutConstraint(item: imageView, attribute: .Top,
                relatedBy:.Equal,toItem:label,attribute:.Bottom,multiplier:1.0,
                constant: 20.0),
                NSLayoutConstraint(item: imageView, attribute:
                NSLayoutAttribute.CenterX, relatedBy: NSLayoutRelation.
                Equal, toItem: view, attribute: NSLayoutAttribute.
                CenterX, multiplier: 1, constant: 0),

                ])
            }
        }
    }
```

In the viewWillAppear() method we are setting the background color. Then if we have a valid Medication object, we create and display a label and image with medication properties being displayed on the label and imageView.

Now press Command+R to run the application. Navigate to the Care Card and view each of the new card detail views. Note that the Care Card detail view is already provided and wired up by CareKit. You should see the results as shown in Figure 4-6.

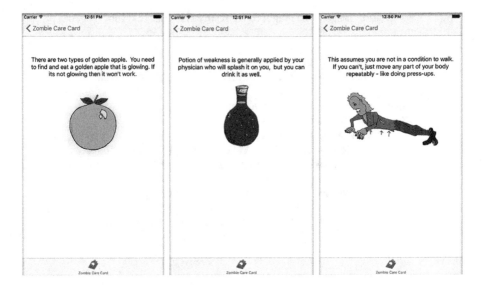

Figure 4-6. *Custom Care Card details view*

Summary

In this chapter we've built and presented the default Care Card ViewController. You learned how to customize its appearance by changing the tint colors, mask images and added an image to the details ViewController. At the end of the chapter you learned how to add some additional custom data on your activity and display this data in a custom detail ViewController.

In the next chapter you will learn more about the System and Measurement Tracker scene.

CHAPTER 5

■ ■ ■

Symptom and Measurement Tracker

In this chapter we will take a detailed look at the Symptom and Measurement Tracker views. We'll extend the ZombieCare app by adding assessment activities and retrieving feedback from the user.

Chapter 1 introduced you to the Symptom and Measurement Tracker module, and you learned that CareKit provides the OCKSymptomTrackerViewController. This controller and its associated views behave in a similar manner to the Care Card ViewController in that it automatically loads activities. However, the similarity ends there. In the Symptom and Measurement module there is no detail view. When a user selects an activity, they must be presented with a view that leads the user through a task to complete their assessment on the activity.

You will learn how to present the default OCKSymptomTrackerViewController and allow it to update automatically from the Care Plan Store. You will add tasks based on a couple of different ResearchKit tasks and steps, capture the results, and store the results in the Care Plan Store. Then you will add a second custom feedback controller. The ResearchKit task will also demonstrate how results can then be added and synchronized with HealthKit.

Before progressing, take note of a few technical design changes within the application. Open the project provided in \chapter5_start. This chapter introduces a new design pattern called Flow Controllers. This is a useful design pattern that prevents controllers from needing to know about each other and helps reduce the amount of logic we place in ViewControllers. The design is implemented by introducing Coordinators and their respective delegates. The Coordinators take responsibility for deciding which interface to present and interacting with the ViewControllers in that interface. In the example app, the new Coordinators are located in the group called Coordinators, and all navigation will in future be handled by them.

© Christopher Baxter 2016
C. Baxter, *Beginning CareKit Development*, DOI 10.1007/978-1-4842-2226-3_5

Build and Present a Symptom and Measurement Tracker

The steps for creating a Symptom and Measurement Tracker scene are similar to creating a Care Card, though it involves using an extra delegate object.

The assessment activities for this chapter are already part of your ZombieCare Plan and are already being loaded into the Care Plan Store. Follow the steps in this section to create and present the OCKSymptomTrackerViewController.

Open ZCCareKitTabCoordinator.swift from the project navigator. Add the following method below the createCareCardViewController() method:

```
private func createSymptomtrackerViewController() ->
OCKSymptomTrackerViewController {
        let viewController = OCKSymptomTrackerViewController(carePlanStore:
        carePlanManager.store)

        // Setup the controller's title and tab bar item
        viewController.title = NSLocalizedString("Zombie Assessment",
        comment: "")
        viewController.tabBarItem = UITabBarItem(title: viewController.
        title, image: UIImage(named:"symptoms"), selectedImage:
        UIImage(named: "symptoms-filled"))
        viewController.showEdgeIndicators = true;

        return viewController
}
```

Now call this method from the start() method. Add the following code after the call to createCareCardViewController() and update the line below to include the symptomTrackerController in the tab bars ViewController array:

```
let symptomTrackerController = createSymptomtrackerViewController()
tabbarcontroller.viewControllers = [UINavigationController(rootViewController:
careCardViewController),
UINavigationController(rootViewController: symptomTrackerController)]
```

That's it. Press Command+R and you will see the new Symptom Tracker view presented in the activities in the tab (see Figure 5-1).

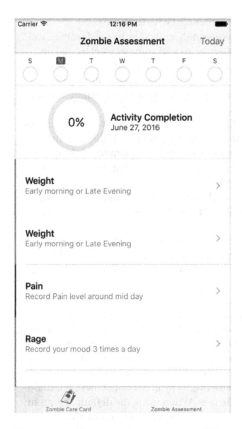

Figure 5-1. *The Default Symptom and Measurement Tracker view*

Let's have a closer look at the view to see what is there.

Reviewing What's Been Presented

In a similar manner to the Care Card, you will see the Week Day and overall assessment completion progress. The progress tint color currently defaults to blue, which you can change by simply setting the tint color as before. Let's do that quickly. In the createSymptomTrackerViewController() method, add the following line before returning the controller:

```
viewController.progressRingTintColor = UIColor.MaskTintColor()
```

The tint color will now display green so it's consistent with the Care Card.

Below the progress indicator is the list of assessment activities. In the ZombieCare Plan there are some activities specified as daily activities and some as weekly, and on some days of the week there are multiple occurrences. So CareKit interprets the number of occurrences on the shown date, but instead of a circular button representing each occurrence or event of the activity on a single row, this view presents a separate row for each occurrence.

The reason for this is because the user will need to see the results of each assessment task individually and, of course, to activate the assessment task views independently too.

At this stage you cannot see the result because we haven't implemented the delegate yet. You will, however, see what appear to be duplicate items in the list. This highlights a problem with the ZombieCare Plan we specified.

As you've learned already, an activity has a schedule, and this schedule specifies the number of occurrences of an activity for a day. This is the same for daily or weekly schedules.

In the case of the ZombieCare Plan, the daily schedule for the Weight activity has been set to 2. And the Rage weekly task has three items scheduled for each day of the week. When CareKit generates the relevant events for each occurrence, it simply creates multiple instances of OCKCarePlanEvents where required for each day.

One might argue that this a limitation in CareKit when defining activities. It would probably be more useful to be able to specify multiple time values for each event. For example, If there were 2 events on a day, one might occur at 8 a.m. in the morning and another at 5 p.m. This would, of course, add a complication when defining events for an activity, so Apple simplified it and specified the number of events only. However, each event does include a property to indicate the index of its occurrence.

The Symptom Tracker view only orders these events by index but shows no visual indication of that, which can be confusing to the user. When using the default Symptom Tracker controller it seems appropriate, therefore, to only specify a separate singular activity for each event where required
(each activity has one occurrence regardless of whether it is a daily or weekly schedule).

Let's modify the ZombieCare Plan accordingly. Replace the list of assessment activities with the following JSON:

```
"assessment_activities": [
                        {
                        "identifier": "004",
                        "group_identifier": "",
                        "title": "Weight",
                        "color": "Gold",
                        "text": "Early morning or Late Evening",
                        "startdate": "20160531T120000+0000",
                        "scheduletype": "Daily",
                        "schedule": "1",
                        "task": {
                        "identifier": "Task1",
                        "steps": [
                                {
```

```
                "identifier": "001",
                "title": "Input your weight",
                "format": "Quantity",
                "unit": "lb"
                }
                ]
    }
},
{
"identifier": "005",
"group_identifier": "",
"title": "Pain",
"color": "Purple",
"text": "Record Pain level around mid day",
"startdate": "20160531T120000+0000",
"scheduletype": "Weekly",
"schedule": "1,1,1,1,1,1,1",
"task": {
"identifier": "Task1",
"steps": [
                {
                "identifier": "001",
                "title": "How was your pain today?",
                "format": "Scale",
                "maxvaluedescription": "Very high",
                "minvaluedescription": "Very low",
                "maxvalue": 10,
                "minvalue": 1,
                "defaultvalue": -1,
                "stepvalue": 1,
                "vertical": false
                }
                ]
    }
},
{
"identifier": "006",
"group_identifier": "",
"title": "Morning Rage",
"color": "Orange",
"text": "Record your mood in the moring",
"startdate": "20160531T120000+0000",
"scheduletype": "Weekly",
"schedule": "1,1,1,1,1,1,1",
"task": {
"identifier": "Task1",
"steps": [
```

```
                              {
                              "identifier": "001",
                              "title": "On a sale of 1 to 10, how
                              do you rate your temper?",
                              "format": "Scale",
                              "maxvaluedescription": "Very Angry",
                              "minvaluedescription": "Calm",
                              "maxvalue": 10,
                              "minvalue": 1,
                              "defaultvalue": -1,
                              "stepvalue": 1,
                              "vertical": false
                              }
                              ]
                    }
                    },
                    {
                    "identifier": "007",
                    "group_identifier": "",
                    "title": "Midday Rage",
                    "color": "Orange",
                    "text": "Record your mood at midday",
                    "startdate": "20160531T120000+0000",
                    "scheduletype": "Weekly",
                    "schedule": "1,1,1,1,1,1,1",
                    "task": {
                    "identifier": "Task1",
                    "steps": [
                              {
                              "identifier": "001",
                              "title": "On a scale of 1 to 10, how
                              do you rate your temper?",
                              "format": "Scale",
                              "maxvaluedescription": "Very Angry",
                              "minvaluedescription": "Calm",
                              "maxvalue": 10,
                              "minvalue": 1,
                              "defaultvalue": -1,
                              "stepvalue": 1,
                              "vertical": false
                              },
                              {
                              "identifier": "002",
                              "title": "On a scale of 1 to 10, how
                              irrated are you?",
                              "format": "Scale",
                              "maxvaluedescription": "Very
                              Irritated",
```

```
                            "minvaluedescription": "Not Much",
                            "maxvalue": 5,
                            "minvalue": 1,
                            "defaultvalue": -1,
                            "stepvalue": 1,
                            "vertical": false
                            }
                            ]
            }
        },
        {
        "identifier": "008",
        "group_identifier": "",
        "title": "Evening Rage",
        "color": "Orange",
        "text": "Record your mood in the evening",
        "startdate": "20160531T120000+0000",
        "scheduletype": "Weekly",
        "schedule": "1,1,1,1,1,1,1",
        "task": {
        "identifier": "Task1",
        "steps": [
                            {
                            "identifier": "001",
                            "title": "On a sale of 1 to 10, how
                            do you rate your temper?",
                            "format": "Scale",
                            "maxvaluedescription": "Very Angry",
                            "minvaluedescription": "Calm",
                            "maxvalue": 10,
                            "minvalue": 1,
                            "defaultvalue": -1,
                            "stepvalue": 1,
                            "vertical": false
                            }
                            ]
        }
        }
        ]
```

In this case, the Weight activity is set to one per day, and we've created separate activities for recording Rage levels at different intervals in the day.

It's not ideal, but I wanted to highlight how you as the developer need to take care when defining the Care Plan, and at least things should be a little clearer to the user now.

In the next section you will learn how to implement the OCKSymptomTrackerViewControllerDelegate and present a ResearchKit task.

Implementing the ResearchKit Task ViewController

The OCKSymptomTrackerViewControllerDelegate protocol defines two methods. An object that adopts this protocol is responsible for presenting the appropriate controller to perform an assessment. It also allows the object to modify or update the events before they are displayed.

The didSelectRowWithAssessmentEvent() function tells the delegate when the user selected an assessment event. The willDisplayEvents() function tells the delegate when a new set of events is fetched from the Care Plan Store.

In this section you will learn how to adopt the protocol and display a ResearchKit task when a user selects an activity.

Refactoring the Assessment Activity Models

Before implementing the delegate, the data model needs to be refactored to better support the loading of assessment activities and their steps. You can find the updated model code in the chapter_05_start folder.

Let's look at what's changed and what's been added:

- The activity protocol and struct has been refactored now to use protocol extensions to implement the correct behavior for an intervention activity.

- An assessment protocol, extension, and struct have been added to provide assessment-specific behavior, such as for creating assessment activities and tasks and parsing the assessment-specific JSON.

- An ActivityStep protocol and extension have been added to support loading the specific activity step JSON.

- The CarePlan has a new helper method called findAssessmentActivity to get an assessment based on its identifier.

- careplan.json has been cleaned up so we can demonstrate loading different style assessment activities and steps.

Now that you're up to date with the model changes, we can continue to add support to load a ResearchKit Assessment task and then store the results. The steps are as follows:

1. Implement the OCKSymptomTrackerViewControllerDelegate didSelectRowWithAssessmentEvent() method and present the ResearchKit ORKTaskViewController.

2. Implement the ORKTaskViewControllerDelegate didFinishWithReason() method to retrieve the task results.

3. Build an OCKCarePlanEventResult from the task results
    and store this along with the updated state of the
    OCKCarePlaneEvent in the Care Plan Store.

4. Dismiss the ORKTaskViewController and view the updated
    results in the OCKSymptomTrackerViewController.

5. Add the HealthKit capability to the application, as this is
    required by ResearchKit.

Presenting the Task View Controller

You can follow these steps by making the necessary changes to Chapter05_start or, if you
prefer, just open Chapter05_final and follow through.

Open the ZCCarePlanTabViewController.swift file and add the following extension to
the end of the file:

```
extension ZCCarePlanTabViewController :
OCKSymptomTrackerViewControllerDelegate {

    func symptomTrackerViewController(viewController:
    OCKSymptomTrackerViewController, didSelectRowWithAssessmentEvent
    assessmentEvent: OCKCarePlanEvent) {

        // Lookup the assessment the row represents.
        guard let sampleAssessment = self.careplanManager?.carePlan.
        findAssessmentActivity
        (assessmentEvent.activity) else { return }

        /*
        Check if we should show a task for the selected assessment event
        based on it's state.
        */
        guard assessmentEvent.state == .Initial ||
            assessmentEvent.state == .NotCompleted ||
            (assessmentEvent.state == .Completed && assessmentEvent.
            activity.resultResettable) else { return }

        // Create an assessment task and `ORKTaskViewController` for the
        assessment's task.
        let taskViewController = ORKTaskViewController(task:
        sampleAssessment.createTask(), taskRunUUID: nil)
        viewController.navigationController!.presentViewController(taskViewC
        ontroller, animated: true, completion: nil)

    }

}
```

The preceding extension handles the `didSelectRowWithAssessmentEvent()` event from the OCKSymptomTrackerViewControllerDelegate.

First, it loads the assessment activity instance for the selected assessment event (OCKCarePlanEvent). It validates that the event is in the correct state. Note that it also checks for the resultResettable property. We'll discuss this in more detail shortly.

The next step creates a ResearchKit ORKTaskViewController. The initializer for this controller takes an instance of a ResearchKit ORKTask object.

Setting the Symptom Tracker Delegate

At this point, the application will not compile because we still need to add support to the assessment activity to create a task. We'll do that next, but first note that the TabBarController needs to be set to be its delegate and then present the ORKTaskViewController instance via the navigation controller.

■ **Note**   ResearchKit provides a series of models and controllers that can be used to collect information from a user for the purposes of a clinical study. There are numerous types of tasks a user might be presented with, and ResearchKit supports a variety of tasks, from collecting signatures and filling out forms to performing active tasks such as monitoring a user walking. ORKTaskViewController presents these tasks modally. If you're not familiar with ORKTaskViewController, you may need to further read up on ResearchKit here `http://researchkit.org/docs/Classes/ORKTaskViewController.html`.

Open the ZCCareKitTabCoordinator.swift file and add the following line in `start()` after the call to `createSymptomTrackerViewController()`:

```
symptomTrackerController.delegate = tabbarcontroller
```

This assigns the TabBarController to be the delegate object for the SymptomTrackerViewController.

Adding a ResearchKit Task

In this section you'll learn how to create a ResearchKit task which can be used by the supporting views. Open Assessment.swift. At the top of the file, change the assessment protocol to the following by adding the `createTask()` method declaration:

```
protocol Assessment : Activity {

    var taskIdentifier : String  { get set }
    var steps : [ActivityStep] {get set}
    func createTask() -> ORKTask
}
```

Now add the following implementation to the Assessment extension:

```
func createTask() -> ORKTask {

        var steps : [ORKQuestionStep] = []

        for step in self.steps {

            let stepidentifier = NSLocalizedString(step.stepIdentifier,
            comment: "")
            let stepquestion = NSLocalizedString(step.question, comment: "")

            var answerFormat : ORKAnswerFormat?

            switch step.format {

            case .Quantity:

                let quantityType = HKQuantityType.quantityTypeForIdentifier
                (HKQuantityTypeIdentifierBloodGlucose)!
                let unit = HKUnit(fromString: step.unit)
                answerFormat = ORKHealthKitQuantityTypeAnswerFormat(quantity
                Type: quantityType, unit: unit, style: .Decimal)

            case .Scale:

                // Get the localized strings to use for the task.
                let maximumValueDescription = NSLocalizedString(step.
                maxValueDescription, comment: "")
                let minimumValueDescription = NSLocalizedString(step.
                minValueDescription, comment: "")

                // Create a question and answer format.
                answerFormat = ORKScaleAnswerFormat(
                    maximumValue: step.maxValue,
                    minimumValue: step.minValue,
                    defaultValue: step.defaultValue,
                    step: step.step,
                    vertical: step.vertical,
                    maximumValueDescription: maximumValueDescription,
                    minimumValueDescription: minimumValueDescription
                )
            }
```

```
        let questionStep = ORKQuestionStep(identifier: stepidentifier,
        title: stepquestion, answer: answerFormat)
        questionStep.optional = false

        steps.append(questionStep)

    }

    // Create an ordered task with a single question.
    let task = ORKOrderedTask(identifier: activityType.rawValue, steps:
    steps)

    return task
}
```

The createTask() method will return a ResearchKit ORKTask instance.

The ZombieCare Plan has specified that each assessment activity can have a single task, and each task can have one or more steps. There are two types of question/answers supported:

- A question with a quantity answer—that is, the answer is a value between two other values, where the min and max values are specified.

- A question with a single value input that specifies a unit of measurement.

By specifying these two different answer types, ResearchKit will display the appropriate task form.

The createTask() method creates an array of ORKQuestionSteps that are passed as a parameter to the ORKOrderedTask initializer.

It is possible that you may want to support alternative question types and even different tasks. You can implement other types of ResearchKit tasks or even create your own. To do that, you will need to define the structure of your data differently and adapt your model and methods appropriately.

You should now be able to build and run the application. Press Command+R and run the app in the simulator. Navigate to the Symptom Tracker tab and select one of the assessment events. You should be presented with the ResearchKit ORKTaskViewController and the relevant task view. You will notice, however, that the view will not close at this stage. That's because you haven't yet implemented the ORKTaskViewControllerDelegate.

Handling Task Completion

Open the ZCCarePlanTabViewController.swift and scroll down to the didSelectRowWithAssessmentEvent() delegate handler. Add the following delegate assignment after the line that creates the ORKTaskViewController:

```
taskViewController.delegate = self
```

Now add the ORKTaskViewControllerDelegate extension code and the completeEvent helper method to the bottom of the file:

```
private func completeEvent(event: OCKCarePlanEvent, inStore store:
OCKCarePlanStore, withResult result: OCKCarePlanEventResult) {
    store.updateEvent(event, withResult: result, state: .Completed) {
    success, _, error in
        if !success {
            print(error?.localizedDescription)
        }
    }
}


extension ZCCarePlanTabViewController: ORKTaskViewControllerDelegate {

    func taskViewController(taskViewController: ORKTaskViewController,
    didFinishWithReason reason: ORKTaskViewControllerFinishReason, error:
    NSError?) {
        defer {
            dismissViewControllerAnimated(true, completion: nil)
        }
    }
}
```

If you run the app now, you will find you can close the task view after having completed the task.

In the next section you will retrieve the result from the task and create a CareKit OCKCarePlanResult that can be associated with the assessment event and stored in the Care Plan.

Creating Assessment Activity Results

Add the following code in the task delegate handler after the defer block so the handler looks like the following:

```
    func taskViewController(taskViewController: ORKTaskViewController,
    didFinishWithReason reason: ORKTaskViewControllerFinishReason, error:
    NSError?) {
        defer {
            dismissViewControllerAnimated(true, completion: nil)
        }
        guard reason == .Completed else { return }

        guard let navController = self.viewControllers?[1] as?
        UINavigationController,let symptomTrackerViewController =
        navController.viewControllers[0] as? OCKSymptomTrackerViewController
        else { return }
```

```
    guard let assessmentEvent = symptomTrackerViewController.
    lastSelectedAssessmentEvent,
    let assessment = self.careplanManager?.carePlan.findAssessment
    Activity(assessmentEvent.activity) else { return }
    let carePlanResult = assessment.buildResultForCarePlanEvent
    (assessmentEvent, taskResult: taskViewController.result)
    completeEvent(assessmentEvent, inStore: (self.careplanManager?.
    store)!, withResult: carePlanResult)
}
}
```

The defer keyword ensures that the ORKTaskViewController will be dismissed
regardless of when this method completes. This is very useful when you have multiple
guard statements that return.

After the defer statement, there are a few guard calls that return if the event has
not been completed. The assessment activity instance is then retrieved using the
findAssessmentActivity() method from the CarePlan class, and this is followed up by a
call to a new assessment method called buildResultForCarePlanEvent().

The buildResultForCarePlanEvent() returns a new instance of a CareKit
OCKCarePlanEventResult object. You need to add this method to the assessment
extension as follows:

```
func buildResultForCarePlanEvent(event: OCKCarePlanEvent, taskResult:
ORKTaskResult) -> OCKCarePlanEventResult {
    guard let firstResult = taskResult.firstResult as? ORKStepResult,
    stepResult = firstResult.results?.first else { fatalError("Unexpected
    task results") }

    if let scaleResult = stepResult as? ORKScaleQuestionResult, answer =
    scaleResult.scaleAnswer {
        return OCKCarePlanEventResult(valueString: answer.stringValue,
        unit'string: "out of 10", userInfo: nil)
    }
    else if let numericResult = stepResult as? ORKNumericQuestionResult,
    answer = numericResult.numericAnswer {
        return OCKCarePlanEventResult(valueString: answer.stringValue,
        unit'string: numericResult.unit, userInfo: nil)
    }
    fatalError("Unexpected task result type")
}
```

The assessment event is then updated in the Care Plan Store with the associated
result (Figure 5-2).

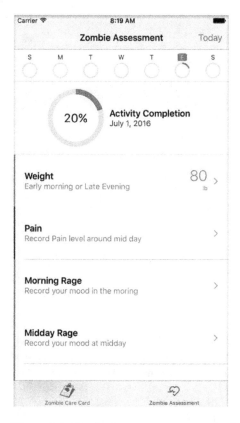

Figure 5-2. *Displaying assessment event results*

At this stage, if you run the application you will find that when you complete a task, the event is updated as stated and the user interface is returned to the SymptomTrackerViewController, which now displays the result adjacent to the event.

There are now only two things left to do: add the Healthkit capability and discuss the resultResettable property.

Adding HealthKit Capabilities

Because we've included ResearchKit and tasks that require using HealthKit quantity units, it's a requirement to include the HealthKit entitlement to the app.

Select the ZombieCare project and target in Xcode and select the Capabilities tab. From here you can turn on HealthKit, as shown in Figure 5-3.

Figure 5-3. *Turning on HealthKit capabilities*

How to Retake Assessments

As promised, here's one final note on the resultResettable property. You may recall this was checked when the selection of an event was handled in the SymptomTrackViewController and the handler returned if this was set to true:

```
guard assessmentEvent.state == .Initial ||
        assessmentEvent.state == .NotCompleted ||
        (assessmentEvent.state == .Completed && assessmentEvent.
        activity.resultResettable) else { return }
```

The resultResettable is a property of OCKCarePlanActivity that specifies whether or not to allow the user to retake the assessment. It defaults to no and is only used by .Assessment activities. In the ZombieCare app, this has been set to true for all activities, so a user can retake the assessment task, but it can be adjusted depending on the requirements.

Updating the Symptom and Measurement Tracker

As you learned in the previous section, by updating the underlying data in your Care Plan Store, the SymptomTrackerViewController updates automatically. This is for free—you don't need to change anything.

Under the hood, the SymptomTrackerViewController subscribes to changes in the store by conforming to the OCKCarePlanStoreDelegate just like the Care Card did. When a change event is signalled, it then fetches the latest events and updates the user interface accordingly.

Integrating Results with HealthKit

CareKit, ResearchKit, and HealthKit all focus on sharing health information. HealthKit itself provides a structure for storing health information that can be shared between apps while protecting a user's privacy.

As we acquire health data in CareKit, it makes a lot of sense to be able to share it with HealthKit so it's only stored once, securely, and potentially the information can be used by other apps. For instance, some common data fields like weight or temperature are supported by HealthKit.

About HealthKit Integration

CareKit provides support for creating HealthKit-related OCKCarePlanEventResults based on HealthKit data. Depending on your requirements you can create results with the following HealthKit types:

- *HKQuantitySample object*: Represents a piece of data with single numeric value, such as height, weight, heart rate, or calories. You must provide a supported HKUnit type.

- *HKCorrelation object*: Groups multiple data entries in a single data entry. Note, though, that CareKit only supports the HKCorrelationTypeIdentifierBloodPressure Correlation type in 1.0.

- *HKCategorySample object*: Describes samples whose values are represented by predefined enumeration values, such as sleep data, which has an enumeration for sleep analysis.

■ **Note**   You can find out more about HealthKit sample types from Apple's documentation.

The way in which CareKit associates an OCKCarePlanEventResult with HealthKit data is through the UUID and sample type properties on an HKSample object. When you create an instance of an HKSample with HealthKit, you specify the sample or quantity type in the initializer. HealthKit will generate a UUID at the time of construction. For example:

```
let quantityType = HKQuantityType.quantityTypeForIdentifier(HKQuantityType
IdentifierBodyMass)!
let quantity = HKQuantity(unit: unit, doubleValue: weightAnswer.doubleValue)
let now = NSDate()
let sample = HKQuantitySample(type: quantityType, quantity: quantity,
startDate: now, endDate: now)
```

Now when you create an instance of an OCKCarePlanEventResult with the preceding sample, CareKit will store the HKSample and HKUnit information and will also set properties for the sample UUID and sample type. When it comes time to load events for an activity, the Care Plan Store will query the Health Store for all the HealthKit samples using the sampleUUID and date and then will use those samples to instantiate the OCKCarePlanEvent and OCKCarePlanEventResult object. Otherwise, it falls back to the default initializers.

▪ **Note** A lot of different sample types and units can be used with HealthKit. You will need to read the HealthKit documentation to understand what relevant types to use for your application.

You will learn next how to integrate your ZombieCare data with HealthKit. To do so, you need to make a few technical choices on how you might determine whether an activity should or can be saved to the HealthStore.

Integrating HealthKit with the Example

The approach taken by the OCKSample application that comes with CareKit uses protocols for some hard-coded activity types. In particular, it creates a protocol called HealthSampleBuilder, which is adopted by the Weight assessment activity. In the Zombie example, it's a little more difficult because we are loading data dynamically and using a more generic implementation for our activities.

The logic used to determine whether one of the Zombie activities can be saved to the HealthKit store is based on inspecting the format field of the assessment task steps. If the step is of type .Quantity, we will assume that a valid unit is provided.

▪ **Note** HKUnit only supports a predefined list of strings. It will throw an exception if you use an invalid string.

The logical place to save data to the Health Store is in the ORKTaskViewControllerDelegate `didFinishWithReason()` method you worked on earlier. You will modify the method to include support for storing results in the HealthKit store. To do so, follow these steps:

1. Check whether the assessment event can be stored in HealthKit.

2. Create a HealthKit sample from the assessment task result.

3. Create an instance of the HealthKit store and request authorization from the user.

4. If authorized, attempt to save the sample to the store.

5. Finally, update the CareKit store with the result.

Adding Support for HealthKit Data

Prior to completing the preceding steps, it is necessary to add a few helper methods to the assessment object, which can generate some of the additional data required.

After the `buildResultForCarePlanEvent()` method in the Assessment extension, add the following:

```
func supportsHealthKit() ->Bool {

        guard let firstStep = self.steps.first as? ZCActivityStep else
        {return false}
        if firstStep.format != .Quantity {
            return false
        }

        return true
}

func getHKQuantityType() -> HKQuantityType {

        guard let firstStep = self.steps.first as? ZCActivityStep else
        {fatalError("Unable to retrieve Task step")}

        var quantityType : HKQuantityType

        switch firstStep.unit {
            case "lb":
                quantityType = HKQuantityType.quantityTypeForIdentifier(HKQu
                antityTypeIdentifierBodyMass)!
        default:
                fatalError("unit not supported")
        }

    return quantityType

}

func getHKUnit() -> HKUnit {

        guard let firstStep = self.steps.first as? ZCActivityStep else
        {fatalError("Unable to retrieve Task step")}

        return HKUnit(fromString:firstStep.unit)
}
```

```
func buildHKSampleWithTaskResult(result: ORKTaskResult) ->
HKQuantitySample {
    guard let firstResult = result.firstResult as? ORKStepResult,
    stepResult = firstResult.results?.first else {
    fatalError("Unexpected task results") }

    let now = NSDate()
    let quantityType = getHKQuantityType()
    var numericAnswer : Double = 0

    if let scaleResult = stepResult as? ORKScaleQuestionResult, answer =
    scaleResult.scaleAnswer {
        numericAnswer = answer.doubleValue
    }
    else if let numericResult = stepResult as? ORKNumericQuestionResult,
    answer = numericResult.numericAnswer {
        numericAnswer = answer.doubleValue
    }

    let hkUnit = self.getHKUnit()
    let quantity = HKQuantity(unit: hkUnit, doubleValue: numericAnswer)

    return HKQuantitySample(type: quantityType, quantity: quantity,
    startDate: now, endDate: now)
}

  func localizedUnitForSample(sample: HKQuantitySample) -> String {

    let formatter = NSMassFormatter()
    formatter.forPersonMassUse = true
    formatter.unit'style = .Short

    let value = sample.quantity.doubleValueForUnit(self.getHKUnit())
    let formatterUnit = NSMassFormatterUnit.Pound

    return formatter.unit'stringFromValue(value, unit: formatterUnit)
}
```

These methods provide support for the following:

- supportsHealthKit(): Returns a bool to indicate if this assessment result can be stored in the HealthKit store.

- getHKQuantityType(): Returns the appropriate HKQuantityType of the given activity steps unit string.

- getHKUnit(): Return an HKUnit for the assessments unit string.

- `buildHKSampleWithTaskResult()`: Creates an HKQuantitySample from the task result that can be stored in the HealthKit store.

- `localizedUnitForSample()`: Returns localized unit string for the given assessment unit that be used when saving the sample to the HealthKit store.

Creating HealthKit Data

Finally, we can now add support to the didFinishWithReason delegate method in ZCCarePlanTabViewController.swift. Scroll down to the bottom and replace the call to completeEvent() with the following code:

```
if assessment.supportsHealthKit() {
        let sample = assessment.buildHKSampleWithTaskResult(taskViewCont
        roller.result)
        let sampleTypes: Set<HKSampleType> = [sample.sampleType]
        let healthStore = HKHealthStore()
        healthStore.requestAuthorizationToShareTypes(sampleTypes,
        readTypes: sampleTypes, completion: { success, _ in

            if !success {
                self.completeEvent(assessmentEvent, inStore: (self.
                careplanManager?.store)!, withResult: carePlanResult)
                 return
            }

        healthStore.saveObject(sample, withCompletion: { success, _ in
                if success {
                    let healthKitAssociatedResult =
                    OCKCarePlanEventResult(
                        quantitySample: sample,
                        quantityStringFormatter: nil,
                        displayUnit: assessment.getHKUnit(),
                        displayUnit'stringKey: assessment.localizedUnit
                        ForSample(sample),
                        userInfo: nil
                    )

                    self.completeEvent(assessmentEvent, inStore:
                    (self.careplanManager?.store)!, withResult:
                    healthKitAssociatedResult)
                }
```

```
                    else {
                        self.completeEvent(assessmentEvent, inStore: (self.
                        careplanManager?.store)!, withResult: carePlanResult)
                    }
                })
            })

        }
        else {
        completeEvent(assessmentEvent, inStore: (self.careplanManager?.
        store)!, withResult: carePlanResult)
        }
```

This completes the steps mentioned earlier to now store the assessment task results in HealthKit and fallback to storing the details in the CareKit store. All the preceding code is in the chapter05_final/ZombiCare.workspace.

If you run the application now using Command+R, navigate to the weight assessment task and complete the task. You will be prompted to authorize the use of the HealthKit store, after which the data is stored and the view is dismissed.

■ **Note** When you've authorized HealthKit once, you will not be prompted unless you reinstall the application.

That completes the section on HealthKit integration. Generally the process of saving to HealthKit is quite easy. The trickier technical decisions will be how you determine what can be saved and formatting the data appropriately as you've seen.

Implementing a Custom Feedback Controller

In previous sections, you've seen how to integrate ResearchKit and HealthKit to prompt a user with tasks to assess the progress of their treatment. ResearchKit has a considerable number of well-thought-out tasks including the standard Ordered or Navigable Stepped tasks and also the Active tasks. These are pretty flexible too, with multiple answer formats, so I recommend understanding your choices first before writing a set of custom tasks.

But you may not be able to use one of these supported tasks for one reason or another. Perhaps they don't exist, or maybe you need to style and present the tasks differently? In this section you will learn how to create a simple task that you can use and plug in to your own application.

There are a couple of approaches you might take when creating your own custom task:

- Create your own custom task by subclassing ResearchKit ORKActiveStep and ORKActiveStepViewController.

- Create your own bespoke task from scratch with your own ViewController and task results.

You now have a good understanding of how to implement a ResearchKit task, so we'll skip that option and learn how to create a task from scratch without the ResearchKit support. If you're interested in custom ResearchKit tasks, you may want to read further on the ResearchKit API documentation.

In the ZombieCare application, the custom task will be a cognitive brain test for the Zombie. It will test to see whether the zombie understands what is food and what is not food based on a series of pictures presented in a Tinder style swipe selector. I think the less accurate a zombie is, the more affected by the zombie virus they are.

For this task, it's best to follow through the solution already implemented in the Chapter_05_final source code.

Defining a Custom Task

To support the Tinder style selection, we've included a set of classes that originated from a Swift open source project.

■ **Note** Open source Tinder style code was created by Richard Kim, which you can find here (https://github.com/cwRichardKim/TinderSimpleSwipeCards). This was subsequently ported to Swift by Brandon Gao (xhttps://github.com/reterVision/TinderSwipeCardsSwift).

In the Xcode project, navigate to the CareTab/BrainTest group. You will find OverlayView, DraggableView, and DraggableViewBackground. These are the base files for implementing the swipe feature. The files have been modified slightly to be a bit more task specific and to include a couple of new structs we want to specify: the cards and task results. BrainTask and TaskResult structs have been added:

- *BrainTask*: Hold the information for a card, including the image to display and the expected result.

- *TaskResult*: Used to record the results form the user's selection.

The DraggableViewBackground class has been modified to be more task specific and has a new delegate added so it can notify delegates when all the cards have been swiped:

```
func didCompleteSwiping(view: DraggableViewBackground) -> Void
```

BrainTestViewController is the main task controller and it's the class that will be instantiated when presenting the task to the user in replacement of the ResearchKit tasks used earlier. It has a simple delegate to indicate when the task is complete in a similar way to previous task controllers:

```
func didFinishWithResult(result: TaskResult)
```

Now that the project is using a different type of task controller, there needs to be a way to identify which controller to use for which class. There's a number of different approaches one might take. For this example, we're simply going to use the groupIdentifier property on Activity to distinguish this task from others. If you look in careplan.json, there is an additional brain assessment task that has been added with the group identifier brain.

Adding the Custom Task

Now that you have an understanding of the supporting classes for the cognitive brain test, let's look at how it's implemented. Open the ZCCarePlanTabViewController.swift file and find the BrainTestViewControllerDelegate extension. This extension is very similar to the other extension for handling ORKTaskViewControllerDelegate. The main difference is that the delegate passes back the TaskResult, which is checked and passed to the Assessment object so it can create a new OCKCarePlanEventResult based on this custom TaskResult.

Finally, in the OCKSymptomTrackerViewControllerDelegate handler in ZCCarePlanTabViewController, we need to decide which task ViewController to load. In our simplistic example, we just check the assessment activities group identifier and load appropriately:

```
if assessmentEvent.activity.groupIdentifier == kBrainGroupIdentifier {

        let taskViewController = BrainTestViewController()
        taskViewController.delegate = self
        viewController.navigationController!.presentViewController(taskV
        iewController, animated: true, completion: nil)
    }
    else {
    let taskViewController = ORKTaskViewController(task: sampleAssessment.
    createTask(), taskRunUUID: nil)
        taskViewController.delegate = self
        viewController.navigationController!.presentViewController
        (taskViewController, animated: true, completion: nil)
    }
```

Press Command+R to view the results in the simulator. Navigate to the Brain Assessment task and swipe to complete the tests. On completion, the view is dismissed, and the results are viewable in the SymptomTrackerViewController (Figure 5-4).

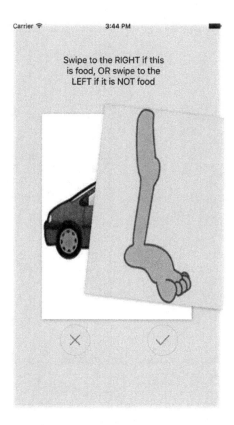

Figure 5-4. Swipe custom task ViewController

There are a number of approaches you might take to customizing your task views. This section demonstrated just one of those. The key items to do are to handle the presentation and completion of the task view and convert the result to a OCKCarePlaneEventResult, which can be recorded in the Care Plan Store.

Summary

In this chapter you've learned more details about CareKit's Symptom and Measurement Tracker scene and how to present it, use ResearchKit tasks, and integrate the results with HealthKit. You also found out how to create and use your own custom task ViewController.

That completes the chapter on the Symptom and Measurement Tracker module. In the next chapter you will learn about the Insights dashboard.

CHAPTER 6

Insights

Chapter 1 briefly introduced you to Insights, and you learned that CareKit provides the OCKInsightsViewController. This controller and its associated views and data types behave quite differently than the previous Care Card and Symptom and Measurement Tracker modules. Unlike activities and events, insights are not stored in the Care Plan Store. In fact, they are not persisted at all, but generated at runtime. They have also been designed to be subclassed to enable developers to present data in their own unique way.

The Insights scene or dashboard is where a user can visualize data related to their care plan. Data can be presented as either messages, such as Tips or Alerts regarding the treatment, or by a chart, which can show the correlation between a treatment plan's intervention and assessment activities. This is where a patient or Care Team can get real value out of CareKit because it enables you to present meaningful analysis. Consider what you can do:

- Visualize the effect of a treatment in relation to the patient's assessment. Does more or less medication have a direct impact on the patient's outcome?

- Display some running commentary on the treatment plan to help incentivize the patient (for example, advise the patient about whether they are adhering to their medication).

- Share the charts and insights with your connections (Care Team, friends, and relatives).

- Provide effective feedback. The Care Team could present additional tips or commentary after reviewing the patient's progress and present this in a message (assuming your Care Plan can be updated remotely).

- Share industry news about a condition, which can be displayed in the messages view.

- Display any arbitrary data using the Insights scene's charts and messages (it's not restricted to CareKit data). You can create insights from any other sources.

© Christopher Baxter 2016
C. Baxter, *Beginning CareKit Development*, DOI 10.1007/978-1-4842-2226-3_6

In addition to all these flexible sources and presentations, as a developer you can also create your own subclasses to present data in your own unique or purposeful way.

The Insights scene provides you with an opportunity to take your Care Plan full circle from treatment and assessment to analysis and presentation of feedback and insights to the patient.

In this chapter you will learn how to implement the Insights dashboard and view insights in both message and chart format. You'll also learn how this scene can be extended to receive feedback from the Care Team with tips on improving the user's condition. The chapter concludes with an inspection of the CareKit Document class and show how this can be shared.

Insight Data Types

Before adding insights to the ZombieCare project, you need to understand the insight data types. CareKit provides the OCKInsightItem abstract class as the base model for items in the OCKInsightsViewController. It has three properties:

- *title*: A string indicating the title of the item

- *text*: A string indicating the description of the item

- *tintColor*: The display tint color of the item

The OCKInsightItem class cannot be instantiated directly because it's an abstract class, but CareKit does include two concrete implementations for messages and charts:

- *OCKMessageItem*: An object that can display text or alerts

- *OCKChart*: An abstract class that provides a model for charts

In addition, CareKit provides the OCKBarChart, a concrete implementation of OCKChart that represents a vertical grouped bar chart, as seen in Figure 1-5 from Chapter 1.

The OCKInsightsViewController displays an array of OCKInsightItem objects. It consists of a UITableView and some custom cell types. One for messages (OCKInsightsMessageTableViewCell) and one for charts (OCKInsightsChartTableViewCell). The controller determines which cell type to use depending on the class type.

An interesting point here is that although the documentation advises that you can use your own concrete subclasses of OCKInsightItem, it's only practically possible to provide a subclass of OCKChart—at least in the current version, which is 1.0 at the time of writing. The reason for this is because the OCKInsightsMessageTableViewCell expects the concrete type OCKMessageItem. Although you might inherit from OCKMessageItem, the cell class will only render the specific OCKMessageItem fields, for example, title, text, and symbol. So it would be pointless to subclass it.

On the other hand, the OCKInsightsChartTableViewCell expects the abstract OCKChart object and renders its view properly along with the title and text properties through polymorphism. You will need to take this into account if you're planning to present some custom insights.

As mentioned earlier, none of these types is included or used by the CareKit Care Plan Store. You will need to provide your own plan on how you utilize these classes in your project and plan how your Insights view will correlate to your Care Plan treatment and assessment activities. Let's first look at how to create messages in more detail.

Creating Messages

Messages can display simple text messages using the OCKMessageItem class. There are two types of messages defined in the OCKMessageItemType enumeration:

- *Alerts*: The Alert message type is defined by the OCKMessageItemTypeAlert. If medication adherence is below a certain threshold, you may want to advise the user using this type.

- *Tips*: The Tip message is defined by the OCKMessageItemTypeTip type. Tips can be provided by the Care Team, for instance, or be based on some analysis of the assessment results.

When displayed, the message type is recognizable by the tint color and symbol appended to the end of the message title.

Apple provides an example with the OCKSample app of a formatted Tip, which indicates a user's percentage adherence to their taking of medication. It's a useful example that demonstrates how a message can convey an insight derived from the data itself. Alternatively, as suggested earlier, the message might actually be retrieved from a server which is updated by the Care Team. Either way, the following code creates a simple message example for an Alert that advises the user if they have missed their medication on the current day:

```
let completedMedicationTasks = 5
let totalMedicationTasks = 7

let message = OCKMessageItem(
    title: "Medication Alert",
    text: "You've only completed \(completedMedicationTasks) out of
    \(totalMedicationTasks) tasks today",
    tintColor: UIColor.redColor(),
    messageType: .Alert)
```

This would look like figure 6-1 when displayed in the Insights view.

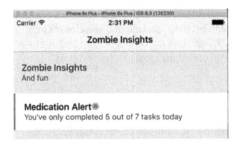

Figure 6-1. *Displaying an OCKMessageItem Alert*

Note how the Alert icon and edge indicator both use the tint color. In the next section you'll learn how to create a chart insight item.

Creating Charts

Creating charts is a good deal more complicated than messages. It requires some considerable thought and planning on how to format the data. There are numerous steps involved to creating a chart.

The most difficult task with respect to creating charts is collecting the data. In some cases this might be from the Care Plan Store, or it may be from another source—for instance, from a remote server. In both cases you'll likely need to make one or more asynchronous calls to the data source and then combine the data using completion handlers. You learned in Chapter 3 how to access data asynchronously from the Care Plan Store, and we'll utilize those methods in this chapter to populate the chart.

Because you will be learning to create an OCKBarChart in this chapter, let's first take a look at the classes provided by CareKit to see how it works.

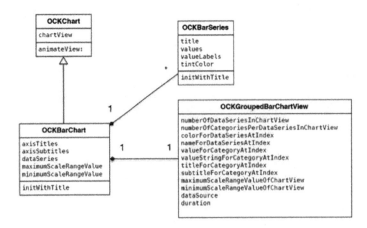

Figure 6-2. *Entity relationship diagram for CareKit charts*

As you can see, OCKChart species two properties:

- *chartView*: This is a UIView and is the method which needs to be overridden to provide a custom chart view.

- animateView(..): This method is called for visible charts to provide a custom animation.

These two properties are used by the OCKInsightsViewController to present the chart.

The OCKBarChart is a concrete subclass of OCKChart and has a number of read only properties for labels and data series. It also has an array of data (dataSeries) represented by OCKBarSeries that is used by a single OCKGroupBarChartView view, which is the concrete chartView.

All the properties are initialized via a custom initializer, initWithTitle(...).

You don't really need to understand the inner details of these classes. You just need to know that when OCKBarChart is initialized, it will take the role of the chartViews data source and coordinate the creation of the chart view using an array of OCKBarSeries and its associated labels.

That means the first step to creating a chart is to define the data series and instantiate one or more OCKBarSeries objects for your chart from your data. For example, the following code demonstrates the creation of two series of data that represent the values collated from the Rage assessment activity results and a medication series taken from the ZombieCare app:

```
let rageBarSeries = OCKBarSeries(
    title: "Rage",
    values: rageValues,
    valueLabels: rageLabels,
    tintColor: UiColor.redColor())

let medicationBarSeries = OCKBarSeries(
    title: "Medication Adherence",
    values: medicationValues,
    valueLabels: medicationLabels,
    tintColor: UIColor.greenColor())
```

Once the series have been defined then the chart can be created as follows:

```
let chart = OCKBarChart(
    title: "Rage",
    text: nil,
    tintColor: UIColor.redColor(),
    axisTitles: axisTitles,
    axisSubtitles: nil,
    dataSeries: [rageBarSeries, medicationBarSeries])
```

The OCKInsightsViewController can now be initialized with an array of insight items that includes the chart.

Now that you've learned the basics of how to create messages and chart insight items, we can take the next step of creating the Insights scene for the ZombieCare app.

ZombieCare App Insights

Your care team will most likely present you with a requirement for some specific and relevant insights along with your care plan. In the ZombieCare app, we will present two messages and a chart.

ZombieCare Message Insights

The following messages are presented:

- *A message Tip*: This will advise the user that if they eat the golden apple before they take the purple potion the medication will be more effective.

- *A message Alert*: A percentage of the medication adherence for *all* medication taken in the previous week will be displayed.

ZombieCare Chart Insights

We will present two data series:

- Series one will represent the average Rage values for each day of the week: the average of the morning, mid-day, and evening Rage values recorded in the assessment view.

- Series two will represent the accumulated medication values for each day of the week: the number of completed tasks for each day of the week.

With this approach, the patient will be able to see a correlation between the medication they've taken and the level of their rage. One would hopefully see that the more the patient adheres to their medication, the lower their temper or rage is, which would indicate the medication is working.

Now that we've defined the data series, we want to visualize in the chart there is one further issue that needs to be addressed. The scale and format of the two data series are different. The medication values for the golden apple, purple potion, and outdoor walk are simple values of 0 or 1 (that is, done or not done), whereas the values range on a scale of between 0.0 and 10.0. To display an accurate and meaningful correlation between the two, one or the other series needs to be adjusted so the series use the same range and scale.

One approach to use is a multiplier to scale or offset the data in one series so it matches the other. For example if the Medication series uses the scale 0.0-1.0, and the Rage scale is based on 0.0-10.0, then we can multiply the medication values by 10 and the scales will be the same.

For the ZombieCare app, this approach will work fine, but we'll also need to use the sum of the daily medication and the average of the assessment result values. For example:

Daily Medication value = SUM(completed Golden Apple + completed potion of weakness + completed outdoor walks)

Daily Rage value = AVERAGE(morning Rage + mid-day Rage + evening Rage)

Now that the requirement has been defined in terms of what insights to display in the Insights scene, an approach to retrieve the data and create the insights that can be used by the InsightsViewController must also be defined.

For the first message insight there is no dependence on data; it's simply a Tip, so we can hard-code it or perhaps load from the ZombieCare plan. But the other message will require us to make a calculation based on the event results of the intervention activities, and the chart will require us to generate some values based on the assessment event results. This data can all be retrieved from the Care Plan Store and converted into InsightItems.

When loading data from the Care Plan Store, it is necessary to ensure that one adheres to certain principles:

- The data must be loaded asynchronously.

- The results should be dispatched back onto the main thread.

- Only load a limited data set.

You learned in Chapter 3 that CareKit provides an API for querying the Care Plan Store. Apple has also provided a nice example of loading data in its OCKSample using some of the CareKit APIs. In the ZombieCare app you will follow a similar approach and base the implementation on Apple's example, from which you'll learn to query the Care Plan Store and convert events and event results into OCKInsightItems.

Creating Insights

The approach taken by Apple's OCKSample app is to use NSOperations, blocks, and queues to query the Care Plan Store and convert the results to InsightItems.

■ **Note**   If you're not familiar or unaware of how NSOperations work, you should read up on Apple's documentation before proceeding.

Let's take a look at at how this works. To begin, take a look at what the implementation actually consists of. There are two key NSOperation subclasses:

- The QueryActivityEventsOperation subclass is used to query the Care Plan Store for Activity Events using the enumerateEventsOfActivity() API method. This operation also has a method for finding events based on the specified activity identifier.

- The BuildInsightsOperation subclass that creates two OCKSInsightItems, an OCKMessageItem, and an OCKChartItem by using a copy of the data queried from the QueryActivityEventsOperation operation.

Another helper class called InsightsBuilder creates, aggregates, and enqueues the preceding two operations and ensures that they run in order by setting their dependencies. Results are then stored in an Insights property, which can then be used by other classes when the completion handler is triggered.

There are a few interesting points to note about this implementation:

- Although the QueryActivityEventsOperation is fairly generic in that it can query for different events based on the activity identifier string, the BuildInsightsOperation is not, because it is creating two very specific Insight items.

- The preceding operation classes make extensive use of the GCD semaphores and queues to coordinate the running of asynchronous queries on the CareKit Plan Store.

- The InsightsBuilder class makes use of the NSBlockOperation operation in order to aggregate the results from the query operations into the BuildInsightsOperation.

- The InsightsBuilder class uses the .addDependency() method to set the dependencies of all operations to ensure that they run in the correct order.

- The completion block is specified only on the last running operation, that is, the BuildInsightsOperation.

The classes under discussion have already been added to the project source code in /chapter_06_start.

In the ZombieCare app you will need to provide the following additional steps:

- Call the InsightsBuilder operations whenever an activity or event is updated in the CareKit Plan Store.

- Provide a mechanism to update the UI when insights have been updated.

You may recall from Chapter 3 that you learned about the ZCCarePlanStoreManager class, which provided a wrapper around the CareKit Plan Store and also received notification when the CareKit Plan Store was updated by implementing the OCKCarePlanStoreDelegate delegate. You will now use this class to be the entry point to using the InsightsBuilder on initialization and also when these updates occur. In addition, it will provide its own ZCCarePlanStoreManagerDelegate.didUpdateInsights() delegate method, which can be used to update the insights property on the OCKInsightsViewController, thereby completing the lifecycle of insights.

This whole process can be a little tricky to follow, especially if you're new to NSOperations, so we'll take it step by step and implement the classes into the ZombieCare app.

The insights differ slightly from the OCKSample. In Apple's example, it is preparing insights for just two specific types of activities, whereas in the ZombieCare app the results required are based on numerous activities. For instance, it's required to measure the percentage medication adherence on *all* .Intervention activities and the average of the Rage values based on *all* the Rage activities.

To facilitate this requirement, a group identifier called rage has been specified and added in the ZombieCare Plan to all Rage activities. This means the app can query the CareKit store using the group identifier.

The insights implementation within the ZombieCare app is based on the Apple example. If you open /chapter06_start, you will find a refactored version of the classes mentioned. The changes include the following:

- The QueryActivityEventsOperation class is initialized with the ZCCarePlanStoreManager and an *array* of activity structs. The main() method has also been refactored from the original example as it iterates through the array of activities, finds the equivalent OCKCarePlanActivity using the ZCCarePlanStoreManager. findActivity() method. Note that a new innersemaphore has been included to help synchronize calls when enumerating activities.

- The BuildInsightsOperation class has a new method to create a message Tip, called createTipMessage(). createMedicationAdherenceInsight() has been refactored slightly to display an Alert OCKMessageItem if there are no completed events. Finally, the the original createBackPainInsight() method has been refactored to createRageInsight(), and this method now calculates the average Rage values for all the events for each day as per the new requirement.

- The InsightsBuilder class remains largely the same. Minor differences include passing an instance of ZCCarePlanStoreManager to the QueryActivityEventsOperation initializer and filtering the activities array so only relevant activities are passed as parameters when initializing.

Building and Presenting the Insights Scene

With the preceding classes in place, it's time to update the source from chapter06_
start to use the classes to create insights and update the project to include the
OCKInsightsViewController. The steps to achieve this include the following:

1. Initialize the InsightsBuilder in the ZCCarePlanStoreManager.

2. Update the OCKCarePlanStoreDelegate functions in
   ZCCarePlanStoreManager so that insights are updated when
   the CareKit Care Plan Store is updated.

3. Add an extension to ZCCareKitTabCoordinator to provide an
   implementation of the ZCCarePlanStoreManagerDelegate so
   it knows when insights are updated.

4. Add a method to the ZCCareKitTabCoordinator to create and
   add the OCKInsightsViewController to the tab.

Start by opening ZCCarePlanStoreManager.swift from the project navigator and find
the init(carePlan:CarePlan) method. Add the following properties above the init method:

```
var insights: [OCKInsightItem] {
      return insightsBuilder.insights
}
private var insightsBuilder: InsightsBuilder
```

Before the call to super.init(), add the following line to initialize the
InsightsBuilder in the init method:

```
self.insightsBuilder = InsightsBuilder()
```

After the super.init() line set the careplanManager property as self so it is the
current instance for ZCCarePlanStoreManager:

```
self.insightsBuilder.carePlanManager = self
```

That completes the first step to initialize an instance of the InsightsBuilder and store
it as a property in ZCCarePlanStoreManager. Now update the OCKCarePlanStoreDelegate
implementation as follows:

```
extension ZCCarePlanStoreManager: OCKCarePlanStoreDelegate {
    func carePlanStoreActivityListDidChange(store: OCKCarePlanStore) {
        updateInsights()
    }

    func carePlanStore(store: OCKCarePlanStore, didReceiveUpdateOfEvent
    event: OCKCarePlanEvent) {
        updateInsights()
    }
}
```

Add the following as the last line in the init(carePlan:CarePlan) method:

```
updateInsights()
```

Now add the `updateInsights()` method immediately after the `cleanStore()` method:

```
func updateInsights() {
        insightsBuilder.updateInsights { [weak self] completed, newInsights in
            // If new insights have been created, notifiy the delegate.
            guard let storeManager = self, newInsights = newInsights where
            completed else { return }
            storeManager.delegate?.zcCarePlanStoreManager(storeManager,
            didUpdateInsights: newInsights)
        }
    }
```

That completes steps 1 and 2. Build the project by pressing Command+B to ensure everything compiles okay.

Now open ZCCareKitTabCoordinator in order to add the ZCCarePlanStoreManagerDelegate and create the Insights ViewController.

At the bottom of the file, include the add the following extension:

```
extension ZCCareKitTabCoordinator: ZCCarePlanStoreManagerDelegate {
   func zcCarePlanStoreManager(manager: ZCCarePlanStoreManager,
   didUpdateInsights insights: [OCKInsightItem]) {
  insightsController!.items = insights
   }
}
```

This extension handles the `ZCCarePlanStoreManagerDelegate`. `didUpdateInsights()` function. In the function it simply sets the Insights parameter to the items property on the InsightsViewController.

At the top of the class add a property for the Insights ViewController:

```
var insightsController  : OCKInsightsViewController?
```

A reference to this property is stored so it can be accessible when the preceding delegate method is called to update the insights on the ViewController.

Now in the init(..) method, add the following to set `self` as the Care Plan manager's delegate:

```
self.carePlanManager.delegate = self
```

It's now possible to build and present the Insights scene. Add the following method to the end of the class:

```
private func createInsightsViewController() -> OCKInsightsViewController {

let viewController = OCKInsightsViewController(insightItems:
carePlanManager.insights, headerTitle: "Zombie Insights", headerSubtitle:
"And fun")

  // Setup the controller's title and tab bar item
  viewController.title = NSLocalizedString("Zombie Insights", comment: "")
  viewController.tabBarItem = UITabBarItem(title: viewController.title,
  image: UIImage(named:"insights"), selectedImage: UIImage(named: "insights-
  filled"))
  viewController.showEdgeIndicators = true;
  return viewController
    }
```

This method is similar to the other creation methods to create and return the Insights ViewController.

Modify the start() method to call createInsightsViewController() and add the controller to the tab as follows:

```
insightsController = createInsightsViewController()
tabbarcontroller.viewControllers = [UINavigationController(rootViewController:
careCardViewController),
                                    UINavigationController(rootViewC
ontroller: sympTomTrackerController),
                                    UINavigationController(rootViewC
ontroller: insightsController!)]
```

That's it. You've now successfully created and added the Insights ViewController to the main care tab. The Insights builder is initialized in the Care Plan manager, and when activities are updated in the Care Plan Store, its delegate is handled so that the insights can be updated and refreshed on the Insights ViewController.

Build and run the project using Command+R. If you immediately navigate to the Insights tab, you should see a couple of default message insights with the Tip and an Alert advising there are no treatments completed. That's because there are no event results from any activities, as the actives are being re-initialized every time the app runs in the simulator.

Figure 6-3. *Default Insights view*

Now try to complete some of the intervention activities and do some of the rage assessment activities for the previous week. You will then see the Tip message and the Alert message above an updated chart, as illustrated in Figure 6-4.

Figure 6-4. *Updated Insights view*

This concludes building, updating, and presenting insights. In the next section, you will learn how to create a document based on the insights and share it.

Creating a Document

CareKit provides a set of classes for creating HTML or PDF documents that can be shared with a Care Team, friends, or family. The document consists of a title, page header, and one or more elements, including:

- Subtitles
- Paragraphs
- Images
- Charts
- Tables

You'll learn how to create a document and add each of these elements in turn. The steps to create document include the following:

1. Creating the document elements

2. Creating the document with the elements

3. Accessing and viewing the document data

It's most likely that you will want to generate a document from the CareKit Connections controller when you're looking to share it with one of your connections, although this may not always be the case.

As you can see, it's also possible to create a document that may contain some elements derived from insights and elements from other sources. It's important therefore to structure the code to make both the document elements and document accessible from different parts of the application, and to generate the document only when required.

The logical place to generate a document in the ZombieCare app is in the ZCCarePlanStoreManager class, because it receives updates from the Insights builder and has a property with all the insights.

The required document elements for the ZombieCare app are as follows:

- Title and a subtitle. The title is simply the name of the Care Plan, and the subtitle should read "The following is an assessment for treatment of Zombiefication."

- Image of the zombie we use in the app, just to demonstrate this element

- Paragraph saying "Below are some insights with respect to the patient's treatment and self-assessment."

- Table of message insights

- Insight chart

- Paragraph with the patient's comments.

- Subtitle called "Summary"

- Summary paragraph with Lorem Ipsum (nonsensical boilerplate language)

- Page header specifying the name, version, and date of the application this document was created from

Open ZCCarePlanStoreManager.swift and scroll to the bottom of the class implementation. Add the following method to generate a document:

```
func generateDocument(comment: String?) -> OCKDocument? {

    var elements: [OCKDocumentElement] = []

    let subtitleElement = OCKDocumentElementSubtitle(subtitle:
    "Assessment for the treatment of Zombification")
    elements.append(subtitleElement)

    let zombieImage = UIImage(named: "Zombie")
    let imageElement = OCKDocumentElementImage(image: zombieImage!)
    elements.append(imageElement)

    if self.insights.count > 0 {

        let introElement = OCKDocumentElementParagraph(content: "Below
        are some insights with respect to the patients treatment and
        self assessment.")
         elements.append(introElement)

        let insightHeaders : [String]? = ["Messages"]
        var insightRows : [[String]]? = [[]]

        for insight in self.insights {
            if insight.isKindOfClass(OCKMessageItem) {
                insightRows![0].append(insight.text!)
            }
        }

        let tableElement = OCKDocumentElementTable(headers:
        insightHeaders, rows: insightRows)
        elements.append(tableElement)

        for insight in self.insights {
            if insight.isKindOfClass(OCKChart) {
                let chartElement = OCKDocumentElementChart(chart: insight
                as! OCKChart)
                 elements.append(chartElement)
                 break;
            }
        }
    }

    let subtitleCommentsElement = OCKDocumentElementSubtitle(subtitle:
    "Patient Comments")
    elements.append(subtitleCommentsElement)
```

```
    if let theComment = comment {
        let commnetsElement = OCKDocumentElementParagraph(content:
        theComment)
        elements.append(commnetsElement)
    }
    else {
        let commentsElement = OCKDocumentElementParagraph(content: "No
        Comments")
        elements.append(commentsElement)
    }
    let subtitleSummaryElement = OCKDocumentElementSubtitle(subtitle:
    "Summary")
    elements.append(subtitleSummaryElement)

    let summaryparagraphElement = OCKDocumentElementParagraph(conte
    nt: "Lorem ipsum dolor sit amet, consectetur adipisicing elit, sed
    do eiusmod tempor incididunt ut labore et dolore magna aliqua. Ut
    enim ad minim veniam, quis nostrud exercitation ullamco laboris
    nisi ut aliquip ex ea commodo consequat. Duis aute irure dolor in
    reprehenderit in voluptate velit esse cillum dolore eu fugiat nulla
    pariatur. Excepteur sint occaecat cupidatat non proident, sunt in
    culpa qui officia deserunt mollit anim id est laborum.")
    elements.append(summaryparagraphElement)

    let document = OCKDocument(title: "Zombie Care Plan", elements:
    elements)
    document.pageHeader = "Zombie Care, Version 1.0, - \(NSDate())"

    return document
}
```

The generateDocument() method is quite self-explanatory. It begins by generating each document element type as specified. Note the table element is generated by iterating through the existing insights and creates a new row item for each message insight.

There is an optional comment added, which allows the patient to add their own comments to the document in its own section. Finally, the document is created with the elements array.

Now open the ZCCarePlanCoordinator.swift file. Replace the empty viewDocument(sender:CarePlanViewController) action with the following implementation:

```swift
func viewDocument(sender: CarePlanViewController) {

        let alertController = UIAlertController(title: "Comments?", message:
        "Add your comments to be included in the document", preferredStyle:
        .Alert)

        let confirmAction = UIAlertAction(title: "Add", style: .Default) { (_) in
            if let field = alertController.textFields?.first {
                self.showDocument(field.text)
            } else {
                self.showDocument("")
            }
        }

        let cancelAction = UIAlertAction(title: "Skip", style: .Cancel) { (_) in
            self.showDocument("")
        }

        alertController.addTextFieldWithConfigurationHandler { (textField) in
            textField.placeholder = "Comment"
        }

        alertController.addAction(confirmAction)
        alertController.addAction(cancelAction)

        self.navigationController.presentViewController(alertController,
        animated: true, completion: nil)
}
```

And now add the method to show the document:

```
func showDocument(comment: String?) {

        if let document = self.carePlanManager?.generateDocument(comment) {
            document.createPDFDataWithCompletion { (PDFData, errorOrNil) in
                if let error = errorOrNil {
                    // perform proper error checking here...
                    fatalError(error.localizedDescription)
                }
                let documentViewController = DocumentViewController(document:
                PDFData)
                    self.navigationController.pushViewController(documentView
                    Controller, animated: true)
            }
        }
        else {
            let alertController = UIAlertController(title: "Error!",
            message: "Document cold not be created", preferredStyle: .Alert)
            let confirmAction = UIAlertAction(title: "Ok", style: .Default)
            { (_) in}
            alertController.addAction(confirmAction)
            self.navigationController.presentViewController(alertController,
            animated: true, completion: nil)
        }
}
```

The viewDocument() method has already been wired up. First it prompts the user to enter a comment (the user can optionally skip this step). The generateDocument() method is then called and once successfully created it is presented in a web view.

Once the preceding code has been added, press Command+R to build and run the application in the simulator. Before viewing the document, enter the Care Plan section and update the treatment and assessment activities for the previous week as you did before. Check the Insights view is updated accordingly and then select Back from the Care Card tab to return to the main view in the app.

Now select View Document. After entering your comment, you should be presented with a view of the document similar to Figure 6-5.

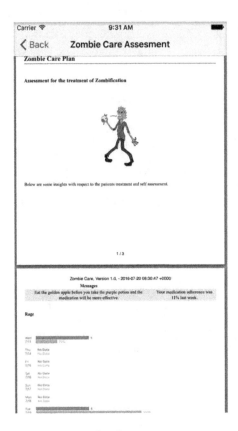

Figure 6-5. *Insights document view*

This demonstrates creating and displaying an OCKDocument instance using most of the elements available. In this example you also learned how to access and view the PDF document data. OCKDocument also has a property called .HTMLContent that provides the document in HTML format.

Now that you've learned how to generate a document from patient insights, the document data is easily accessible and can be shared through any channel you like. For instance, you might post the data to the remote server, email the PDF as an attachment, or even use the HTML data directly in an HTML-formatted email using MFMailComposeViewController.

All the code for everything we've been discussing is located in the /chapter06_final project source code.

Summary

In this chapter you learned about the data types and controllers provided by CareKit to formulate insights related to the patient's treatment and self-assessment. You've learned how to generate insights from the activity event results in the Care Plan Store and display this both in the Insights dashboard/scene and as a PDF document.

In the next chapter you will learn about connections.

CHAPTER 7

Connect

Chapter 1 introduced you to the Connect scene, and you learned that CareKit provided the OCKConnectViewController. This controller and its views are used to display your Care Plan connections and share details of your Care Plan and its insights to them.

In this chapter we will focus on the onboarding of new connections to the sample ZombieCare app and loading in the Care Team connections from the mock service.

The onboarding step will be displayed when the application is first loaded. It integrates with the user's address book to allow the user to select and add connections of their choice. This will be followed by loading and processing of any connections from the Care Plan service.

The user will then be able access their connections, which will be presented in the OCKConnectViewController. You will also learn about the sharing options available to users.

Connect Data Types

Contacts in CareKit are represented by the OCKContact class. The class provides information about the contact and includes the following properties:

- *type*: CareKit defines two types of contacts, .CareTeam and .Personal.

- *name*: A string representing the contact's full name

- *relation*: A string to indicate the relationship of the contact

- *tintcolor*: A tint color used to display the contact details—if not specified, the app tint color will be used

- *phoneNumber*: The contact's phone number (optional)

- *messageNumber*: A phone number used for messaging the contact (optional)

- *emailAddress*: A string used to email the contact (optional)

- *monogram*: A string indicating the monogram for the contact (optional)

- *image*: A string indicating an image name for the contact (optional)

■ **Note**   A contact must have either a monogram or an image of the initializer, or else the OCKContact class will assert. If the image is not provided, then the ContactViewController will expect to find and display a monogram and vice versa.

As with insights, contacts are not loaded into the CareKit Care Plan Store, but instantiated at runtime and passed to the OCKConnectViewController initializer.

Creating Contacts

The following code demonstrates how to create a single Care Team contact:

```
let contact = OCKContact(contactType: .CareTeam, name: "Holly
Helpful", relation: "Nurse", tintColor: UIColor.greenColor(),
phoneNumber: CNPhoneNumber(stringValue: "888-555-5512"), messageNumber:
CNPhoneNumber(stringValue: "888-555-5512"), emailAddress: "helpful@
zombiecare.com", monogram: "HH", image: "holly")
```

In this example all properties have a valid value, but you can set the optional properties to 0 if required. Notice also that the phone and message numbers are represented by the CNPhoneNumber object. CNPhoneNumber is a class provided by Apple's ContactsUI framework.

Onboarding Contacts

Now that you've got an understanding of the CareKit contact data types and how to create a CareKit contact, it's time to learn how to onboard contacts in the ZombieCare app. The process of doing this includes numerous steps, as follows:

1.   Create a struct to represent Contact data in the app.

2.   Load contacts from the careplan.json into the ZombieCare Plan.

3.   Add a new ConnectionsViewController, storyboard, and flow coordinator for the onboarding views. Then modify the initial ZCAppCoordinator to load this when the app first runs.

4.   Provide support in the ConnectionsViewController to access the Contacts database and select new contacts, which are then added to the Care Plan.

5.   Update the app to use these classes and present the onboarding views when it starts or when selected from the main view.

Once these steps have been completed, the app will be ready to present the CareKit Connections scene.

Adding and Loading Contact Data

Start by loading the project source code in /chapter_07_start into Xcode. You will find that there are some classes that have been prepared and added to support the loading of contacts.

Open contact.swift from the Model group in the project navigator. This class follows a similar pattern as activities but represents a contact. There are a couple of key differences:

1. There are two custom initializers, one to initialize a contact from JSON that will be used to load data from the service, and another to initialize a contact from a ContactUI CNContact class, which will be used when selecting a contact from the user's Address book.

2. There is a function called createCareKitContact that returns an instance of an OCKContact object.

The ZCContact struct will provide you a concrete Contact object that can be used within the application.

Let's complete steps 1 and 2 by providing support within the app to load and store the contacts in the app's Care Plan. Open CarePlan.swift and add the following property to hold the list of contacts:

```
var connections : [Contact] = []
```

Now add the following two functions to the end of the struct implementation:

```
func allCKContacts()-> [OCKContact] {
        let ckcontacts = connections.map( {
        $0.createCareKitContact()
        })
        return ckcontacts
}

    mutating func AddContact(contact : ZCContact) {
        self.connections.append(contact)
}
```

The first function, allContacts(), returns an array of CareKit OCKContact objects by using the map function to convert the list of ZCContact objects. The second function is a mutating function that lets you add contacts to the existing list.

Now, in the CarePlan ZCAPIResponse extension initializer, add the following code after the loop that adds assessment activities:

```
if let contacts = json["connections"] as? Array<NSDictionary> {
        for contact in contacts {
            let contact = ZCContact(json: JSON(contact))
            connections.append(contact)
        }
    }
```

This loop parses the array of connections from the given JSON, creates an instance of an ZCContact object for each one, and adds them to the list of connections in the Care Plan. By adding the preceding, the Care Plan now supports the loading of all connections from the careplan.json file. Check that the app builds by pressing Command+B.

Adding the Onboarding Views

For the next step, the project has already been prepared with some classes to support onboarding. The classes in the Connections group include the following:

- *ConnectionsViewController*: The onboarding ViewController to be loaded when the application is initially started. This ViewController provides a simple implementation to guide the user into selecting more contacts from the iOS Contacts database.

- *Connections.storyboard*: A storyboard to represent the UI for the ConnectionsViewController.

Following is the class in the Coordinators group:

- *ZCOnboardingCoordinator*: This class is similar to other coordinators and is responsible for the flow of loading and dismissing the onboarding views.

Let's have a look at each class in more detail to get a better understanding of how contacts are loaded. Although not necessarily specific to CareKit, it helps to have a basic understanding of the classes implementation before adding support to the app to use them.

ConnectionsViewController and Connections.storyboard

This ConnectionsViewController manages a single view that represents the ZombieCare app's onboarding. The associated view in the connections.storyboard is quite simple in that it just prompts the user to select contacts and has a label to display how many contacts were selected. The user can tap the Done button, which calls the ConnectionsViewControllerDelegate to pass the selected contacts to the Care Plan and closes the view.

To select contacts, this view controller will load the Contacts CNContactPickerViewController and handle its delegate methods to receive the selected contacts—or Cancel. Note that the app must first request access to the Contacts UI before it can be used.

This example suffices for the purposes of this book, but you should take into consideration a couple more points:

- In a real production app, you will probably want the ability to display and edit the list of selected contacts. The sample application does not provide this feature and does not prevent duplicates from being added.

- CareKit requires some additional fields that are not in the Contacts database (or potentially some other source) as you may have noted in the OCKContact data type. For instance, relation, color, and monogram. It might be useful to provide a way to edit selected contacts to set these properties directly.

- In the Contacts database there are numerous different keys and fields for phone numbers and addresses. You may need to adjust this to your requirements if you use it.

The ConnectionsViewControllerDelegate provides two methods:

- didSelectContacts(..): Is called when the view is closed and passes the list of selected contacts to the coordinator, which acts as the delegate handler.

- didCancel(...): Is called when the Contacts view is cancelled.

ZCOnboardingCoordinator

The ZCOnboardingCoordinator class has the same responsibilities as other coordinators and follows the same pattern for loading the onboarding ViewController and storyboard with the start() function. It also handles the ConnectionsViewControllerDelegate methods.

The didSelectContacts(..) handler takes responsibility for adding the selected contacts to the ZombieCare Plan. It loops through the list of CNContact contacts and calls the careplan.AddContact() function, which converts each one to a ZCContact object and stores it in the app's Care Plan. The handler then calls its own delegate method to close the view.

That covers the onboarding implementation. You will now provide support within the ZombieCare app to use these classes. There are a lot of code changes coming up, so if you prefer you can refer to the final source of this chapter if you get stuck.

Add the Onboarding

The final step to making use of the onboarding classes involves some refactoring of the ZCAppCoordinator. This includes modifying the initial startup code to switch between loading the onboarding views or the main app view and implementing the ZCOnboardingCoordinatorDelegate delegate methods.

Launching the Onboarding Views

Open the ZCAppCoordinator.swift file from the project navigator. Replace the class declaration with the following code to include the ZCOnboardingCoordinatorDelegate:

```
public class  ZCAppCoordinator : ZCOnboardingCoordinatorDelegate ,
ZCCarePlanCoordinatorDelegate, ZCCareKitTabCoordinatorDelegate {
...
```

Replace the showMainView() functions with the following code:

```
private func showMainView()->Void {

        if(self.carePlanManager == nil ) {
        let service = newZCService(.Mock)
           let mockResource = MockResource(path: "careplan", method: "GET",
           headers: nil, parameters: nil)

          service.request(mockResource) { (response : CarePlan?, error) in
             if error == nil {
                  self.carePlanManager = ZCCarePlanStoreManager(carePlan:
                  response!)
                  self.loadView()
              }
              else {
                  fatalError("Plan failed to load")
              }
          }
        }
        else {
            loadView()
        }
    }
```

Then add these two new methods after the showMainView() function:

```
func loadView() {
    if self.onBoardingDisplayed == false {
        self.loadOnboardingView()
    }
    else {
        self.loadCarePlanView()
    }
}

private func loadOnboardingView() {

    let onboardingCoordinator = ZCOn-boardingCoordinator
    (navigationController: self.rootViewController)
    onboardingCoordinator.delegate = self
    onboardingCoordinator.carePlanManager = self.carePlanManager

    self.childCoordinators.removeLastObject()
    self.childCoordinators.addObject(onboardingCoordinator)

    onboardingCoordinator.start()
}
```

The showMainView() function has been modified to call the new function loadView(). The new function loadView() includes some simple logic to switch between calling the loadOnboardingView() or the loadCarePlanView().

It's possible you'll require some more sophisticated loading logic or even persist the state of the application in NSUserDefaults, but this example is sufficient to demonstrate the ZombieCare app requirement.

The new loadOnboardingView() function is very similar to the loadCarePlanView() but differs in that it uses the ZCOnboardingCoordinator class instead.

Closing the Onboarding

You can now implement the ZCOnboardingCoordinatorDelegate. Add the following to the end of the class implementation:

```
func didCloseOnboarding(sender: ZCOnboardingCoordinator) {
    onBoardingDisplayed = true
    self.rootViewController.viewControllers.removeAll()
    self.start()
}
```

This delegate handler sets a flag to indicate that the user has finished with the onboarding and then reloads the views.

Load the Onboarding View from the Care Plan

The last part of the puzzle is to enable the user to load the onboarding views from the Main Care Plan view. This will enable the user to access and add more contacts to the Care Plan at any time.

Open the CarePlanViewController.swift file and replace the CarePlanViewControllerDelegate class with the following:

```
protocol CarePlanViewControllerDelegate: class {
    func didBuidCareCard(sender: CarePlanViewController)
    func viewDocument(sender: CarePlanViewController)
    func selectContacts(sender: CarePlanViewController)
}
```

This just adds a new function selectContacts(..). Then replace the selectContacts() IBAction, which has already been wired up to the storyboard, with this code:

```
@IBAction func selectContacts(sender: AnyObject) {
    delegate?.selectContacts(self)
}
```

Now open ZCCarePlanCooridnator.swift and you can add support for the updated CarePlanViewControllerDelegate. Add the following function after the viewDocument() function:

```
func selectContacts(sender: CarePlanViewController) {
    self.delegate?.didSelectContacts(self)
}
```

This function is the implementation for the selectContacts delegate function. It defers the method onto to its on delegate handler. Then replace the ZCCarePlanCoordinatorDelegate with the following:

```
protocol ZCCarePlanCoordinatorDelegate {
    func didClose(sender: ZCCarePlanCoordinator)
    func didSelectContacts(sender: ZCCarePlanCoordinator)
}
```

Next you will need to uncomment a few lines of code in the ZCOnboardingCoodinator. swift file. Open the file, find the didSelectContacts method, and uncomment the loop that adds contacts to the Care Plan.

Finally you can now set up the selectContacts delegate handler in the ZCAppCoordinator. Open ZCAppCoordinator and at the end of the class implementation add this handler:

```
func didSelectContacts(sender: ZCCarePlanCoordinator) {
    self.rootViewController.viewControllers.removeAll()
    self.loadOnboardingView()
}
```

That completes all the changes you need to make. The user can now select a button on the Main Care Plan view to restart the onboarding step, and the new delegates enable us to handle the switching of the views.

Press Command+R to build and run the application in the simulator. The first view you see should be the main onboarding view (Figure 7-1).

Figure 7-1. *The initial onboarding view*

This view represents the ConnectionsViewController for onboarding.

To add one or more contacts from the address book, select the button, and you should be presented with a contacts view like the one shown in Figure 7-2.

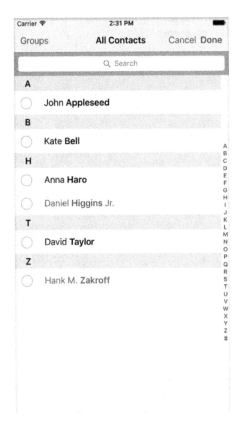

Figure 7-2. *The contacts picker view*

The CNContactPickerViewController allows the user to select one or more contacts.

■ **Note** The first time a user runs the app they will be prompted to request access to the Contacts database. Once allowed, the request box will not be displayed again.

Users can tap Cancel to close the view without selecting any contacts or Done to add any selected ones.

Select a couple of contacts and tap the Done button. The
CNContactPickerViewController view will close, and the previous onboarding view will
now be displayed, as shown in Figure 7-3.

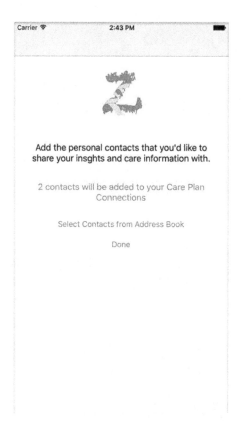

Figure 7-3. The updated onboarding view reflects how many contacts have been selected

As you can see, the view has been updated with a label that indicates the number of
contacts selected, and a Done button is now selectable. As mentioned previously, this view
in a real production app could do with a more detailed table or collection view and allow
the user to modify the contact details.

At this stage the selected contacts have not been added to the ZombieCare Plan. To
do that, select the Done button. When the Done button is tapped, the selected contacts are
added to the ZombieCare Plan and the onboarding view is then closed. The user is then
navigated back the Main Care Plan view (Figure 7-4).

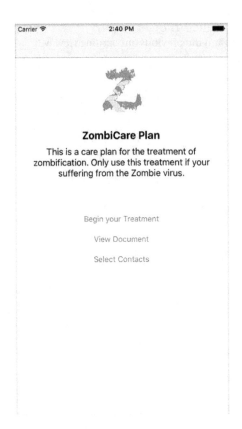

Figure 7-4. *The Main Care Plan view is displayed after contacts have been added*

At this stage it's a little difficult to see what's changed, but if you look at the Xcode debug view (Figure 7-5), you can see some printouts for each contact added.

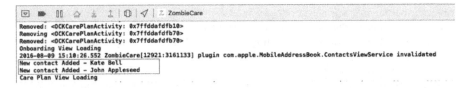

Figure 7-5. *Debug view of added contacts*

This concludes the section on onboarding new contacts into the ZombieCare app.

Now that you've successfully loaded the Care Team and some personal contacts into the ZombieCare Plan, you will be able to display these contacts in the CareKit Connect scene.

Presenting the Connect ViewController

The apps contacts are now safely stored in the Care Plan in a property array called connections. In this section you will learn how to add the CareKit Connect scene to the Care tab and interact with the contacts displayed.

As with the other CareTabs previously added, there is just one step required to include a Connect tab: add support to the ZCCareKitTabCoordinator to add the CareKit OCKConnectViewController.

In the project navigator open ZCCareKitTabCoordinator.swift file and add the following function at the end of the class implementation:

```
private func createConnectViewController() -> OCKConnectViewController {
    let viewController = OCKConnectViewController(contacts:
    carePlanManager.carePlan.allCKContacts())
    viewController.title = NSLocalizedString("Zombie Connections",
    comment: "")
    viewController.tabBarItem = UITabBarItem(title: viewController.
    title, image: UIImage(named:"connect"), selectedImage: UIImage(named:
    "connect-filled"))
    viewController.showEdgeIndicators = true;
    return viewController
}
```

Now replace the start() function with the following:

```
func start() {
    //Load the TabBarcontroller from the storyboard
    let storyboard = UIStoryboard(name: "CareTab", bundle: nil)
    let tabbarcontroller = storyboard.instantiateViewControllerWith
    Identifier("TabBarController") as! ZCCarePlanTabViewController

    tabbarcontroller.careplanManager = self.carePlanManager

    // Create the Care Card Viewcontroller
    let careCardViewController = createCareCardViewController()
    careCardViewController.delegate = tabbarcontroller

    //Create the Symptom tracker Viewcontroller
    let sympTomTrackerController = createSymptomTrackerViewController()
    sympTomTrackerController.delegate = tabbarcontroller
```

```
//Create the Insights Viewcontroller
insightsController = createInsightsViewController()

//Create the Connect Viewcontroller
let connectionController = createConnectViewController()

//Load all the controllers into the tab bar. note the care card
viewcontroller must be in a navigation controller
tabbarcontroller.viewControllers = [UINavigationController
                                    (rootViewController:
                                    careCardViewController),
                                    UINavigationController
                                    (rootViewController:
                                    sympTomTrackerController),
                                    UINavigationController(rootView
                                    Controller: insightsController!),
                                    UINavigationController(rootView
                                    Controller: connectionController) ]

//Display the Tab bar with the care card
self.navigationController.presentViewController(tabbarcontroller,
animated: true, completion: nil)
}
```

The createConnectViewController() function instantiates the
OCKConnectViewController and passes the array of OCKContact objects from
the Care Plan to the controller's initializer. The start() method now calls the
createConnectViewController() function and adds the controller to the tab's controller
array.

That's it. You are now able to run the app in the simulator by pressing Command+R.
Run through the steps to add a few contacts and then select the Begin your Treatment
button from the Main Care Plan view. Once displayed, you should be able to select the
Zombie Connections tab.

The first thing to note about the Connect scene is that it now displays the two separate
sections for the Care Team and Friends & Family, as shown in Figure 7-6.

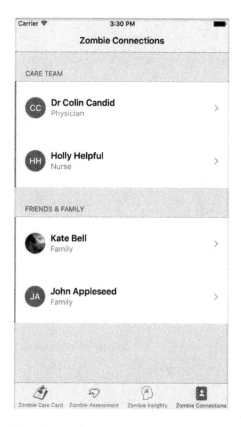

Figure 7-6. The CareKit Connect scene with contacts loaded

Note also that in your version, you may not have an image for the personal contacts you selected, and only the monogram will be displayed. If you want to test and see a contacts image, you will need to run the Contacts app in the simulator and edit one of the contacts you selected to add their image. If you then rerun the app and select the contact, you should see their image in the Connect scene.

Next select one of your contacts to view their details. You should be presented with a view similar to Figure 7-7.

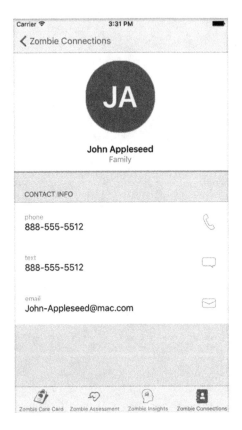

Figure 7-7. The CareKit Contact details view

As you can see, the details view now includes the contact's contact details, and, depending on their properties, there should be Call, Message, and Email options to enable the user to contact that person directly. All the logic for these actions is handled internally by the CareKit OCKConnectionViewController.

There is just one key thing missing from the details view now: the Sharing option enables you to share data with the contact. You will learn how to add this in the next section.

Sharing Insights with Connections

The CareKit framework provides support for sharing data with the contacts listed in the Connect module. It provides support for this by way of a delegate.

The OCKConnectViewControllerDelegate is provided with two delegate functions:

- `didSelectShareButtonForContact(..)`: Tells the delegate when the user selected the share button for a contact.

- `titleForSharingCellForContact(..)`: Asks the delegate for the title to be shown in the sharing cell for a contact.

Adding sharing support to the ZombieCare app is quite trivial. First, set the delegate for the OCKConnectViewController in the ZCCareKitTabCoordinator by adding the following line after creating the OCKConnectViewController in the start function, so it looks like this:

```
let connectionController = createConnectViewController()
connectionController.delegate = tabbarcontroller
```

This sets the TabBarController to be the delegate in the same way we did for the Care Card and Symptom Tracker.

Now add the delegate extension to the tab bar implementation. Open ZCCarePlanTabViewController.swift, scroll to the bottom, and add the following extension code to the end of the file:

```
extension ZCCarePlanTabViewController : OCKConnectViewControllerDelegate {

    /// Called when the user taps a contact in the
    `OCKConnectViewController`.
    func connectViewController(connectViewController:
OCKConnectViewController, didSelectShareButtonForContact contact: OCKContact,
presentationSourceView sourceView: UIView) {
        let document = self.careplanManager?.generateDocument("")
        document!.createPDFDataWithCompletion { (PDFData, errorOrNil) in
            if let error = errorOrNil {
                // perform proper error checking here...
                fatalError(error.localizedDescription)
            }
            let activityViewController = UIActivityViewController(activityIte
            ms: [PDFData], applicationActivities: nil)
            self.presentViewController(activityViewController, animated:
            true, completion: nil)
        }
    }
}
```

The extension provides an implementation for the `didSelectShareButtonForContact()` delegate method. The code first calls the `generateDocument()` method from the Careplan Manager class to generate a document based on the users insights. On success, it then creates a PDF which is then loaded into an UIActivityViewController for sharing.

In this example there is limited error handling because it simply demonstrates how to share the patient's insight document that you learned to generate in previous chapters. Note also that you're not limited to generating or sharing insights only. In fact, you can create any form of data you like and also share it using other mechanisms, such as by calling some API with the data. It all depends on your requirements and the resources available in your application.

Run the app in the simulator using Command+R and after going through the steps of adding contacts again navigate to a contact's detail view. It should include the Sharing section, as shown in (Figure 7-8).

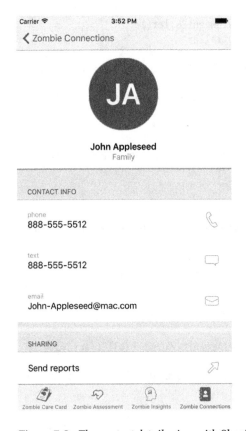

Figure 7-8. *The contact details view with Sharing options*

Finally, if you select the Sharing button, you will be presented with the UIActivityViewController, as demonstrated in Figure 7-9. As you can see, it includes some default options on the simulator to share: Mail, Copy, or Print. You may want to experiment on an actual device to share the Insights PDF using other options.

Figure 7-9. *The UIActivityViewController*

■ **Note** If you try and share on the simulator using the Mail option, the MailCompositionService throws an exception and quits—so try running on a device.

This concludes the sharing section. We've not implemented the other delegate function, but try it out and change the text title displayed in the Sharing Cell for a contact.

Summary

In this chapter you've learned about the CareKit OCKContact data type, how to load contacts from a Care Plan service or the address book, and how to create new OCKContact objects that can be used by the Connect scene. You then learned how to display the Contact scene with the contacts and share the patient's insights using the UIActivityViewController.

This concludes the key functionality provided by the CareKit framework. By now you should feel confident enough to write your own CareKit applications.

In the next chapter you will learn how to extend your application and integrate it with HealthKit, Apple Watch, and today extensions to make it more useful to the user.

CHAPTER 8

Extending CareKit Apps

In this chapter we'll investigate further options for developers to extend the usefulness of their CareKit apps through integration with HealthKit and developing an Apple Watch app and a Today extension. You will learn how an Apple Watch app can communicate with a CareKit iPhone app and receive notifications. By extending the iPhone app, you will learn how patients can benefit from combining these technologies and therefore improve their after-care experience. The chapter concludes by wrapping up the ZombieCare example application.

HealthKit Primer

HealthKit has been available on the iPhone since iOS 8 and on the Apple Watch since WatchOS 2. This section introduces the reader to the basics of HealthKit integration, but it's not a comprehensive guide to HealthKit itself.

The benefits of each of Apple's healthcare frameworks (HealthKit, ResearchKit, and CareKit) are quite well documented, and there are plenty of blogs where you can read a lot of information about them. What's less understood is how to combine the technologies into a practical solution other than in fitness apps.

With CareKit, this opportunity becomes clearer. With user permissions, you can incorporate HealthKit data into your app's assessments, store or save data to HealthKit so it can be used by other applications, and even retrieve data from the HealthKit data store to use in the Insights Report that users can send to their Care Team. We'll work next to include this functionality into the ZombieCare app.

Note   You can find additional reference documentation and an overview on HealthKit at https://developer.apple.com/reference/healthkit.

In Chapter 5 you learned how to provide some basic HealthKit integration with the Symptom and Measurement Tracker, which stores the weight measurements entered by a user in HealthKit. You may recall there were a few steps involved:

- Authorizing HealthKit

- Storing data in the HealthKit store (weight)

- Synchronizing the CareKit store data with the HealthKit data

In this chapter we will extend the application by adding the following additional data to the Insights Report: age, gender, weight, height, and heartRate. All these items will be of benefit to the Care Team when assessing the patient's condition.

Defining HealthKit Requirements

Open the project source from /chapter_08_HealthKit. In this version of the project you will find there are a few helper classes already added to the project. From the project navigator, find and open ZCHealthManager.swift form the Services/HealthKit group.

ZCHealthManager is a class that provides a number of methods to help authorize the user with HealthKit and query the Health Store for some specific types of data (called age, gender, height, weight, and heartRate).

Next open HKHealthStore+AAPLExtensions.swift. This file contains an extension method on the HKHealthStore called mostRecentQuantitySampleOfType(). This method creates and executes queries for data.

That's all you need in order to authorize and access the specific data required for ZombieCare. For a more sophisticated application, you might want to extend this class with functions to write data to HealthKit or query for other types.

The ZombieCare requirement is to update the Insights document with HealthKit data. To achieve this, you need to complete the following steps:

1. Update the ZCCarePlanStoreManager.generateDocument() method to include the additional parameters for health data and add the health elements to the document.

2. Modify the ZCCarePlanCoordinator.showDocument() function to include calls to the health manager class before generating the document.

3. Refactor the ZCCarePlanTabViewController connection delegate call to ZCCarePlanStoreManager.generateDocument() to pass the new parameters.

Updating to the Insights Document

Begin step 1 by opening ZCCarePlanStoreManager.swift and navigating to the generateDocument() function. Change the signature of the function from this:

```
func generateDocument(comment: String?) -> OCKDocument? {...}
```

To this:

```
func generateDocument(comment: String?, age: Int?, gender:
HKBiologicalSexObject?, height: Double? , weight : Double?, heartRate:
Double?) -> OCKDocument? {...}
```

Doing so enables the function to receive the additional optional values.

Now replace the comment "Add HEALTHKIT data here" in the function with the following code snippet:

```
//Add data from healthKit
      if let theAge = age,
          let theGender = gender,
          let theHeight = height,
          let theWeight = weight,
          let theHeartRate = heartRate {

          let subtitleDetailsElement = OCKDocumentElementSubtitle
          (subtitle: "Patient Details")
          elements.append(subtitleDetailsElement)
          let ageElement = OCKDocumentElementParagraph(content:
          "Age: \(theAge)")
          elements.append(ageElement)
          let genderElement = OCKDocumentElementParagraph
          (content: "Gender: \(genderString(theGender))")
          elements.append(genderElement)
          let heightElement = OCKDocumentElementParagraph(content:
          "Height: \(theHeight)")
          elements.append(heightElement)
          let weightElement = OCKDocumentElementParagraph(content:
          "Weight: \(theWeight)")
          elements.append(weightElement)
          let hrElement = OCKDocumentElementParagraph(content: "Heart
          Rate: \(theHeartRate)")
          elements.append(hrElement)
      }
```

The function is now prepared to accept the HealthKit parameters, and if all fields are available it adds each individual element to the document. Note that the application won't build at this stage until we've completed steps 2 and 3.

Fetching Additional HealthKit Data

For step 2, open the ZCCarePlanCoordinator.swift file and navigate to the showDocument() function. Replace the function with the following new showDocument() function:

```
func showDocument(comment: String?) {
        CMHealthManager.sharedInstance.authorizeHealthKit { (success, error) in
            if error == nil {
                dispatch_async(dispatch_get_main_queue(), {
                    () -> Void in
                    let age = CMHealthManager.sharedInstance.fetchAge()
                    let gender = CMHealthManager.sharedInstance.fetchSex()

let height = CMHealthManager.sharedInstance.fetchHeight()
                    let weight = CMHealthManager.sharedInstance.
                    fetchWeight()
                    let heartrate = CMHealthManager.sharedInstance.
                    fetchHeartRate()
                    print("User stats \(age) - \(gender) - \(height) -
                    \(weight) - \(heartrate)")
                    if let document = self.carePlanManager?.
                    generateDocument(comment, age: age, gender:
                    gender, height: height, weight: weight,
                    heartRate: heartrate) {

                        document.createPDFDataWithCompletion { (PDFData,
                        errorOrNil) in
                            if let error = errorOrNil {
                                // perform proper error checking here...
                                fatalError(error.localizedDescription)
                            }
                            let documentViewController = DocumentView
                            Controller(document: PDFData)
                            self.navigationController.pushViewController
                            (documentViewController, animated: true)
                        }
                    }
                    else {
                        let alertController = UIAlertController(title:
                        "Error!", message: "Document cold not be
                        created", preferredStyle: .Alert)
                        let confirmAction = UIAlertAction(title: "Ok",
                        style: .Default) { (_) in}
```

```
                    alertController.addAction(confirmAction)
                    self.navigationController.presentViewController
                    (alertController, animated: true, completion: nil)
                }
        })
    }
  }
}
```

The function has been refactored to first request the user to authorize the app to access the HealthKit store. If you have a look at the authorizeHealthKit() method in the ZCHealthKitManager class, you will find that it specifically requests read-only permission for the data types required.

Once authorized, the healthStore is queried for each item of data in turn. HealthKit queries are normally asynchronous, meaning that these helper methods have each implemented dispatch semaphores so that the data can be returned synchronously.

Potentially the required data may not have been added to the Health Store, so in this example the functions simply return optional values. Also the functions expect to receive all the data. You may want to optimize this for your requirements.

Once the HealthKit data items have been fetched, the generateDocument method can be called, passing the new parameters.

Refactoring to Include the New Data

Lastly, you will need to update the other call to generateDocument() in the ZCCarePlanTabViewController.swift file. Open the file and find the call to generateDocument().

In this case we will not pass any HealthKit data to the function, so simply replace the function call with the following:

```
let document = self.careplanManager?.generateDocument("", age: nil, gender:
nil, height: nil, weight: nil, heartRate: nil)
```

As you can see, we just pass in nil for all the optional parameters, and this will allow the app to compile. If you prefer, you can add the call to fetch data as we did before.

That completes the steps to support the new HealthKit requirement. Build and run the app by pressing Command+R. Once the app is running, skip the add contacts and select View Document from the main screen.

You will initially be presented with the HealthKit authorization screen shown in Figure 8-1. Select All Categories and then select Allow.

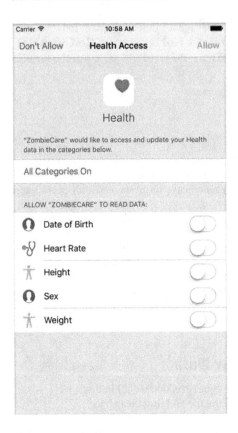

Figure 8-1. *HealthKit authorization screen*

After adding a comment, you will now be presented with the Insights document. At this point you may or may not have the Personal Details data displayed in the report. That depends on whether you have the data in the HealthKit store. If all items are available, then they will be presented as shown in Figure 8-2. However, if any data items do not exist, then the whole section will be missing. You can at this stage decide to either manually enter the data in the HealthKit app, run on a device that includes the data items, or even modify the code you added to display some alternative text if the data is missing—for example, "Not Available".

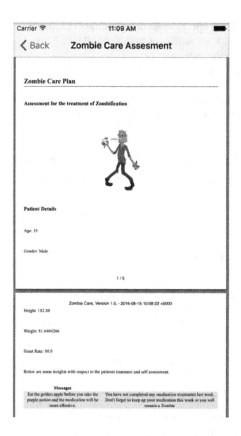

Figure 8-2. *HealthKit data included in the Insights document*

This concludes the section (and example) on integrating HealthKit data into a CareKit application. ZombieCare is just one brief example of how this integration might be applied, but you are only limited by your imagination. You can make use of any of the HealthKit data as long as you request permission for the right data types. On the other hand, any data captured in the application can also be written and shared to the HealthKit data store, which will enable other applications to have access to it.

Today Extensions

Today extensions—or widgets, as they are now called on iOS—give users quick access to information that's important right now. It's easy to see how this can be applicable to patients. Users tend to open the Today view frequently, and with some new focus on extending the lock and home screens in iOS 10, it's a safe assumption to think users might expect the information they're interested in to be immediately available and potentially actionable in those places.

You will learn how to extend the ZombieCare app to present a summary of today's intervention activities and allow the user to mark an activity as being completed. The completed activity will then be updated within the main app.

To demonstrate adding a Today extension to the ZombieCare app, the project has been prepared with a Today extension that includes a new extension target and the ZombieCareWidget project source files. The user interface files have also been prepared so you can focus on the key elements of sharing data to and from the application.

■ **Note**   You can find further information in Apple's documentation on how to add a Today extension at `https://developer.apple.com/library/ios/documentation/General/Conceptual/ExtensibilityPG/`.

Defining the Today Extension Requirement

Begin by opening the project source from the /chapter_08_TodayExtension folder. You will find the new ZombieCareWidget project source files in the group called ZombieCareWidget and a new target called ZombieCareWidget.

Before looking at the files and adding support for sharing data with the extension, let's consider what's required. There are three requirements:

1. To display a list of today's incomplete intervention activity events in the Today extension

2. To enable users to complete an intervention activity event from within the Today screen and update the view

3. To synchronize and view the updated intervention activity events in the main containing application

The key to supporting these requirements is to provide a mechanism for sharing data between the extension and the main application. First, a list of incomplete activities needs to be shared with the Today extension. Then the extension needs to notify the containing app when an activity has been completed.

If you're not familiar with Today extensions, you may find it helpful to read up more information on the architecture of a Today extension before continuing.

Sharing Data with Today Extensions

Even though an app extension bundle is nested within its containing app's bundle, the running app extension and containing app have no direct access to each other's containers (Figure 8-3). One of the approaches recommended by Apple for sharing data is to set up an App group in the target entitlements, and then both the containing app and the extension can use NSUserDefaults to share access to some data.

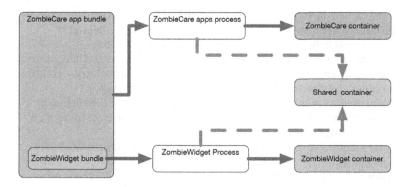

Figure 8-3. *Sharing application data*

This is the approach taken in the ZombieCare app. A new type called ActivityData has been added to the Model group in the project navigator. This class supports being serialized to the NSUserDefaults and includes properties to represent the basic details of an activity, its state, and an identifier to reference its corresponding CareKit Activity and event. The containing app will use two lists for storage: one for the incomplete activities created by the containing app, and another for the completed activities created by the extension.

■ **Note**　It also possible to shared data using other mechanisms such as a shared CoreData store and NSFilePresenter.

Once the data is available within the shared container, the two processes can synchronize their access to the data in order to present the correct information.

Loading and Saving Shared Data

To support the loading and storing of shared data, the ZCCarePlanStoreManager class has been updated with three new functions.

- saveInCompleteActivitiesToSharedStorage(): Converts an array of ActivityData objects to NSData and saves this to the shared storage.

- loadCompletedActivitiesFromSharedStorage(): Loads NSData from shared storage and converts it to a list of ActivityData objects. Once converted, the list of ActivityData objects is passed to another function called updateEvents() for processing. The completed list is then deleted from shared storage.

- updateEvents(): Iterates through the list of completed ActivityData objects, finds the respective CareKit OCKCarePlanEvent object from the Care Plan Store, and updates its status to .Complete.

As mentioned earlier, the project source has already been prepared with the new Today extension target and project source files. All that's required to see the Today extension in action is to call the preceding functions at the appropriate time.

Open ZCAppCoordinator.swift from the main app project navigator and navigate to the `loadCarePlanView()` function. Uncomment the two lines to `loadCompletedActivities FromSharedStorage()` and `saveInCompleteActivitiesToSharedStorage()`.

The `loadCompletedActivitiesFromSharedStorage()` function is called first so it can process all incomplete activities. `saveInCompleteActivitiesToSharedStorage()` is called to save back to storage the fresh list of incomplete activities.

This is all that's required to do for the containing app because the presentation of activities remains the same.

Now open the TodayViewController.swift file from the ZombieCareWidget source files. This file is the main interface controller for the widget. At the top of the file you will find two properties. One is for the list of completed activities, and the other is for the list of incomplete activities. Now scroll down and inspect the `loadData()` function. This function simply loads the incomplete activities from shared storage when the widget is activated.

The user interface for the ZombieCareWidget is just a table that presents a list of the incomplete activities and a button on each row to set the activity to complete. You will see that the tableView DataSource has already been implemented.

Setting the Activity Status

The final step to complete the ZombieCareWidget is to provide the implementation to set an activity to complete. This is done by handling a delegate on the activity row button action.

In the `cellForRowAtIndexPath()` function, uncomment the line that sets the delegate:

```
cell.buttonDelegate = self
```

Now uncomment the TodayViewController extension at the bottom of the same file. This class extension handles the event when a button is tapped in an activity row, which then calls `updateStoredData()`, which in turn marks and saves the completed activity in the shared storage container.

That completes the implementation of both the widget and its containing app to support the sharing of data. There is one final step you need to complete: adding an App group to your project to support shared storage.

Including App Group Capabilities

Select your top level ZombieCare project from the project navigator, choose the ZombieCare target, and then click the Capabilities tab. Turn on the App Groups section and add a group called group.ZombieCare, as shown in Figure 8-4.

Figure 8-4. *Adding the App group*

At this point, you may be prompted to log in to your development portal account, as Xcode will need to update your project entitlements. Once done, select the ZombieCareWidget target and do the same.

That should now complete all the steps for adding the ZombieCare widget. Check that the app compiles by pressing Command+B.

You can test the ZombieCareWidget in the iPhone simulator. To do so, you will need to first run the main app. Ensure that the ZombieCare scheme is selected in the Project Schemes dropdown and run the app using Command+R. This will install and run the new app and extension bundles. The app should look no different than before. Select Skip to bypass the contacts view, and the app will store a list of today's incomplete activity events in the shared storage.

To view the extension, first pull down the Today screen by dragging down with your mouse from the top of the simulator screen. The extension will not yet be displayed because it needs to be installed. Select Edit, add the ZombieCare widget, and then click Done. You should now see the ZombieCare widget displayed with a list of activities, as shown in Figure 8-5.

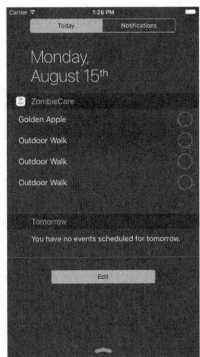

Figure 8-5. *The Today screen before and after completing an event*

Try now to set one of the activities to complete by tapping on ita circular button. If successful, the activity will be removed. You can now close the Today screen.

Once it's closed, you can select Begin Treatment from within the ZombieCare app. You should now see the activity you completed in the Today screen marked also as complete on the main Care Card.

This is a very brief example to demonstrate the usefulness of a Today extension used with CareKit. Your own production solution may well introduce some additional requirements and display other data and fields.

Here are a few key points to take away before developing your own solution:

- You cannot include the CareKit framework and implementation directly within the Today extension because the extension and the container cannot share the same CareKit data store—because they are running in their own separate sandboxed processes.

- You will need to provide support for your own data types to be shared between the processes. These data types need to contain some kind of identifier in order to look up the CareKit objects when synchronizing updates. This is similar to when sharing data with HealthKit, which you learned about when saving weight data with the assessment activities, where CareKit uses a UUID to reference result data.

- There are other options for storing and accessing data, and you will need to provide a mechanism to synchronize the data both ways.

There are many different ways you might present and interact with your CareKit data from a Today extension. This example has merely demonstrated one approach to show what's feasible.

Apple Watch

Like Today extensions, the Apple Watch is also a very useful way to give users quick information about their app and enable them to interact with it in a variety of ways. For instance, you can create glances, notifications, and a Watch app that can also integrate directly with HealthKit. At the time of writing, WatchOS 2 cannot use the CareKit framework, but we are able to communicate with the iPhone application and synchronize data.

In this final section you will learn how to create a simple Apple Watch app for ZombieCare to present a summary of today's incomplete intervention activities and allow the user to mark an activity as being completed, just like the Today extension. In addition, you'll see how to receive notifications from the application.

To demonstrate adding an Apple Watch app for the ZombieCare app, the project has been prepared with a new Apple Watch and Apple Watch extension targets, which include project source code and assets files.

Open the Project workspace from /chapter_08_AppleWatch. You will find two new folders for ZombieCareWatch and ZombieCareWatch extension. Notice also that the ActivityData class file used by the Today extension has also been included in the target membership for the ZombieCareWatch extension.

The requirement for the Watch app is exactly the same as the Today extension, and as before your focus will be on how to share data rather than on the mechanics of building a Watch app. If you've not built an Apple watch app before, then you may want to familiarize yourself with Apple's documentation.

Let's focus initially on the Apple Watch app and then move on to the notifications later.

Apple Watch App

The prepared project you've opened already contains all the source code for loading and displaying a list of ActivityData items, and the UI is all wired up for displaying the data.

Start by opening the InterfaceController.swift file, where you will find a couple of property arrays for holding the complete and incomplete activities. In the updateUI() method, the activities are added to a table view for display.

When the Watch app is activated, the incomplete activities are loaded from local NSUserDefaults storage in a similar way to the Today extension. This is a convenient approach for caching data received from the main iPhone app.

Unlike the Today extension, the Apple Watch does not use a shared storage option with App groups. The reason for this is because as of WatchOS 2, Watch apps run independently in their own process on a physically different device—the Apple Watch. The communication and sharing of data therefore has to be different. The next section talks briefly about how it works.

About Apple Watch Connectivity

A new framework called WatchConnectivity provides bidirectional communications between two processes and lets you transfer data and files in the foreground or background. The framework offers several different options for sending and receiving data, and you need to choose which method is suitable for your application. You will need to read up on the different options, but for the ZombieCare app, the approach taken is as follows.

When sending data from the iPhone app to the Watch app, the updateApplicationContext() method is used. This method can send small amounts of data and is appropriate as it supports background transfers, and the Watch app does not have to be running at the time data is sent.

The Watch app uses a different method called sendMessage(). This method sends data immediately to its counterpart app and can also include a reply handler to check the success of the update, as shown in Figure 8-6.

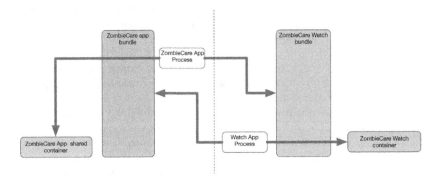

Figure 8-6. *The separate devices communicate using WatchConnectivity and cache the data separately*

When data is received on either the Watch app or the iPhone app, it is cached in NSUserDefaults, and the UI loads the data from this cache.

The iPhone app saves data to the same shared App group (group.ZombiCare) as it did before. This is convenient because the changes can be handled using the same implementation used for the Today extension.

Adding Watch Connectivity to the iPhone App

With this understanding of the general communication channels for sharing data, you can now look at the actual implementation within the project.

In Xcode, find and open WatchSessionManager.swift within the iPhone Apps AppleWatch group folder. This class is a singleton and has three main responsibilities:

1. Initializing and activating a Watch Connectivity session with WCSession

2. Sending data using the `updateApplicationContext()` method

3. Receiving data using the `didReceiveMessage()` method

At the top of the file you will find that session management is handled using some lazy initialization. Below that are the Send and Receive functions.

The `updateApplicationContext()` function loads the incomplete activities from the shared App group.

The `didReceiveMessage()` function is the implementation for the WCSessionDelegate method to receive data that was sent using `SendMessage()` from the watch. When data is received, it simply stores the data in the local shared App group storage container.

When the iPhone application is started, it needs to now initialize the WatchSessionManager. To do this, open the AppDelegate.swift file and in the `didFinishLaunchingWithOptions()` function, uncomment the following line:

```
WatchSessionManager.sharedManager.startSession()
```

In the ZCCarePlanStoreManager.swift file, find and uncomment the `sendDataToWatchApp()` function. This is the function that transmits data to the Watch app.

Now in the ZCAppCoordinator, you can send the data. Open ZCappCoordinator.swift and find the `loadCarePlanView()` function. Uncomment the following line:

```
self.carePlanManager?.sendDataToWatchApp()
```

The iPhone app implementation is now complete and will send data to the Watch app, loading the Care Plan immediately after synchronizing with the Today extension. Note that data will only be sent to the Watch app if it is installed.

Adding Watch Connectivity to the Watch App

Now let's have a look at the Watch app implementation. Navigate to the ZombieCareWatch Extension folder, and you will see a group folder called Communications. In this folder there are two files: WatchSessionManager.swift and Datasource.swift. These two files handle all data comms for the Watch app.

DataSource is a simple struct that unarchives an NSData object into its corresponding array of ActivityData objects. This class is used by the WatchSessionManager and the Apple Watch InterfaceController to handle the data.

The WatchSessionManager, although named the same as the iPhone version described earlier, is similar but different. It is a singleton and has the same responsibilities with respect to initialization, sending, and receiving, but the implementation is different and it includes an additional delegate that will advise when the DataSource has been updated.

When the WatchSessionManager is initialized, it creates an array of DataSourceDelegates. It also provides functions for adding and removing delegates to the array.

In the WatchSessionManager extension, there are three methods including a method for sending data using SendMessage() and another WCSessionDelegate handler for didReceiveApplicationContext(). When the app receives data, it calls all the registered DataSourceDelegates with a copy of the new data.

With this background on the classes provided, let's update the source to make use of these classes. First, open the ExtensionDelegate.swift file and uncomment the line that initializes the WatchSessionManager:

```
WatchSessionManager.sharedManager.startSession()
```

Now open the InterfaceController.swift file. At the top of the file, change the declaration so it conforms to the DataSourceDelegate as follows:

```
class InterfaceController: WKInterfaceController,DataSourceChangedDelegate,
ActivityRowDelegate{
...
}
```

In the WillActivate() function, add the following at the beginning to register with the DataSourceDelegate:

```
WatchSessionManager.sharedManager.addDataSourceChangedDelegate(self)
```

And then add the corresponding call to de-register for updates in the didDeactivate() function.

```
WatchSessionManager.sharedManager.removeDataSourceChangedDelegate(self)
```

Now add the DataSourceDelegate handler at the end of the class as follows:

```
func dataSourceDidUpdate(dataSource: DataSource) {
        if  let activityData = dataSource.activityData
        {
```

```
let sharedDefaults = NSUserDefaults.standardUserDefaults()
NSKeyedArchiver.setClassName("ActivityData", forClass:
ActivityData.self)
    let archiveData = NSKeyedArchiver.archivedDataWithRootObject
    (activityData)
    sharedDefaults.setValue(archiveData, forKey: kActivityData)
    sharedDefaults.synchronize()
    updateUI()
    }
}
```

This function will be called when data is received by the WatchSessionManager as described earlier. It will take the data from the DataSource and cache it locally in NSUserDefaults() before telling the UI to update.

Finally, in the updateStoredData(..) function, add the following code after the call to default.synchonize():

```
let dict = [kCompletedActivityData: completedarchivedObject, kActivityData :
archivedObject]
WatchSessionManager.sharedManager.sendMessageData(dict)
```

The updateStoredData(..) function is called when a user completes an activity. Once the data arrays have been updated and stored locally, a call is made to the WatchSessionManager to send the data to the iPhone application.

That completes the implementation of the Watch Connectivity. Try to build the app using Command+B. If you have any difficulties, you can find the complete implementation in the /chapter_08_final folder.

You can test the ZombieCare Watch in the iPhone and Watch simulators. To do so, you will need to run the main app. First ensure that the ZombieCare scheme is selected in the Project Schemes dropdown and run the app. This will install and run the new app. The app should look no different than before. Select Skip to bypass the contacts view, and the app will store a list of today's incomplete activity events in the shared storage. At this stage, it will not send data because the Watch app has not been installed on the Watch simulator.

Now select the ZombiCareWatch scheme from the project Schemes dropdown and ensure the 48 mm Watch simulator is selected. Select Run, and the Watch simulator will start. You may see a blank screen at this point. If you do, run the iPhone app again in the simulator and then try the Watch app again. When successful, you should see the screen display the list of incomplete activities shown in Figure 8-7. Complete an activity, and the screen should update in the same way we saw on the Today extension.

Figure 8-7. The Watch app before and after completing an event

Switch back to the iPhone simulator. You can now select Begin Treatment from within the ZombieCare app. All going well, you should now see the activity you completed in the Watch app marked also as complete on the main Care Card.

That concludes the demonstration on how to use an Apple Watch app with a CareKit application. This has just been a brief introduction focusing on how to share CareKit data with an Apple Watch. It's more likely that in a production application the Watch app would have more than one display, and you may need to make choices with respect to navigation and what features would make a good Watch app. You may also want to use Glances to display a summary of the user's Care Plan state.

Apple Watch Notifications

Notifications can be incredibly useful for a CareKit application. In the scenario where a patient has a number of treatments or tasks that are scheduled to occur at different times, to get notified about the tasks is a good use of the technology.

By wearing an Apple Watch, a user or patient can receive notifications without opening the iPhone. There are two different types of notifications to consider: push notifications and local notifications. You can implement both or one or the other in your solution. The result on the Watch app is the same—the user will receive the notification and can potentially take further action.

To demonstrate this in the context of a CareKit application, the ZombieCare app will be updated with some local notifications, and you will be able to receive the notification on the Watch app and view the message.

The requirement within the ZombieCare app is relatively simple:

1. When the app launches it will clear any previously set notifications.

2. After the Care Plan is loaded, the app will set new local notifications for each incomplete task. The notifications will be set for mid-day. Where there are multiple occurrences of an activity task, then the app will set one only.

This will suffice for the ZombieCare app, but in a real production app you will likely want to use either push notifications from your Care Plan server or implement a more accurate and specific plan for notification delivery. You will also want to implement a notification for each occurrence of an activity and quite possibly have reminders for other actions too, including assessments. It's also worth remembering that the user may not be running the app every day, and setting notifications in advance may well be a good idea.

Let's begin by continuing to use the same project source as the last section on the Apple Watch app and open the ZCCarePlanStoreManager.swift file. After the function sendDataToWatchApp(), add the following function:

```swift
func postLocalNotifications()  -> Void{

    UIApplication.sharedApplication().cancelAllLocalNotifications()

    let calendar = NSCalendar.currentCalendar()
    let now = NSDate()

    let date = NSDateComponents(date: now, calendar: calendar)
    self.store.eventsOnDate(date, type: .Intervention, completion:
    { (eventsGroupedByActivity, error) in

        dispatch_async(dispatch_get_main_queue(), {

            let midday: NSDate = calendar.dateBySettingHour(12, minute:
            0, second: 0, ofDate: now, options: NSCalendarOptions())!

            for events in eventsGroupedByActivity{
                let activity = events.first!.activity
                for event in events {
                    if event.state != .Completed {
                        let localNotification = UILocalNotification()
                        localNotification.fireDate = midday
                        localNotification.soundName =
                        UILocalNotificationDefaultSoundName
                        localNotification.timeZone = NSTimeZone()
                        localNotification.alertBody = "\(activity.text)
                        is due."
                        UIApplication.sharedApplication().scheduleLocalN
                        otification(localNotification)
                        //we can ignore remainning events as we've set a
                        notification
                        break;
                    }
                }
            }
        })
    })
}
```

161

This function handles both the requirements. First, it cancels any existing notifications. It then iterates over all the current CareKit activities and if it finds an incomplete event it sets up a local notification for mid-day.

Depending on what time you're running through this exercise, you may want to adjust the time set for the notification to a minute or two after the current time for testing purposes.

With this method in place you can now call the function. Open the ZCAppCoodinator.swift file and add the following code after the call sendDataToWatchApp():

```
self.carePlanManager?.postLocalNotifications()
```

Finally, you need to prompt the user to allow notifications by registering for user notifications in the app delegate. Add the following lines to the application didFinishLaunchingWithOptions() function:

```
let types:UIUserNotificationType = ([.Alert, .Sound, .Badge])
let settings:UIUserNotificationSettings = UIUserNotificationSettings(forTyp
es: types, categories: nil)
application.registerUserNotificationSettings(settings)
```

Build and run the application, and notifications will be set. To test notifications you will need to run the app on a physical device. If you don't have an Apple Watch, you can see the result in the simulator by running the ZombieCareWatch(notification) scheme.

■ **Note**   See the AppleWatch documentation to learn about simulating local notifications on the Apple Watch simulator.

This concludes the section on adding local notifications to the ZombieCare app. This has been a simple demonstration on how notifications can enhance your CareKit application. Consider the following as ideas that might be useful for a real production app:

- Include dynamic notification actions that prompt the user to complete an activity. When actioned, the app would load to the appropriate view and the user could then complete the activity.

- Choose a suitable time for your notifications.

- When there is more than one event per activity, only send one notification so the user is not swamped with notifications.

- If you're connecting to a remote Care Plan server, it may be worth implementing server-side push notifications.

- Notifications can also be categorized.

- Make use of notifications badges and sounds.

Those are just a few ideas that might improve an app's user experience. One thing above all is to ensure that notifications are used judiciously so as not to annoy users.

Summary

In this chapter you learned how to integrate HealthKit to extend a CareKit application. You saw that there are multiple reasons for doing this, such as sharing captured data with other applications and leveraging other HealthKit information that can be shared with the user's connections. You also learned how to share CareKit application data with Today extensions and the Apple Watch app, including notifications to engage a user and facilitate their updating of important information.

These are just examples of how you can extend a CareKit app, focused on how to share the data between these different processes and devices. In the next chapter you will learn a little more about how a CareKit application might take advantage of device sensors and other application frameworks and APIs.

CHAPTER 9

Enhancing CareKit Apps

This chapter is about going further with iOS frameworks, features, and capabilities to enhance a CareKit app. CareKit itself is designed to leverage other existing iOS technologies and design patterns, but although the framework does facilitate the process of creating quality treatment apps, a good understanding of app design and other frameworks and tools will help you understand how to best use the framework, incorporate its features into other apps, and go beyond the basic functionality that the framework provides, as demonstrated in Chapter 8.

Apple's iOS SDK includes a large number of frameworks with features and capabilities that can greatly enhance your CareKit application. This chapter highlights a few of these features with examples on how the features can be incorporated in a CareKit app or in an app's assessments or reports that can be shared with a Care Team or other connections.

App Design

iOS apps are generally designed as a series of interconnecting *scenes*. Scenes can be presented in different ways, and we've seen as apps have matured and become quite innovative, a multitude of different animations and innovations come together to provide great user experiences.

CareKit provides a number of these scenes as Care Modules. As we've seen in the CareKit OCKSample application and the ZombieCare app, the examples have focused on presenting these scenes in tabs only.

It's quite likely that your app will contain more than just the CareKit scenes incorporated as part of a broader experience and set of features, which may (or may not) feature tabs. A number of design patterns are available to developers for managing multiple scenes, so learning how to create and combine them is vital when building complex iOS apps.

If you're new to iOS development, consider reading through some of Apple's tutorials. The appendix presents a list of resources you may find useful, including references to Apple's human interface guidelines and programming guides.

© Christopher Baxter 2016
C. Baxter, *Beginning CareKit Development*, DOI 10.1007/978-1-4842-2226-3_9

ResearchKit

Earlier chapters introduced you to ResearchKit, and you learned how to integrate some of its features into a CareKit application. For instance, you learned how an assessment activity can use ResearchKit tasks.

Generally, CareKit and ResearchKit have been developed as complementary frameworks to help simplify the app-creation process, and CareKit does not try to duplicate any ResearchKit features. So it's recommended that CareKit apps incorporate ResearchKit features directly where possible. The examples provided in this book have focused on some simple ordered tasks, however, ResearchKit has many more features that you will find useful.

Task modules range from simple question-and-answer steps and dynamic forms to presenting multiple questions together. There are also multiple-answer formats available, including scaled answers, boolean values, value pickers, image choices, single text choice, multiple text choice, numeric answers, time of day, date, unlimited text, limited text, validated text, email answer, location answer, and vertical scales.

In addition to survey-related tasks, ResearchKit includes Active tasks. Active tasks invite users to perform activities under partially controlled circumstances using iPhone sensors to collect data. These tasks include Motor activities using the accelerometer and gyroscope, Fitness activities like walks using the GPS and gyroscope, cognition tests such as spatial memory, or reaction times using multi touch, accelerometers, and gyroscopes—even voice and audio-related tasks.

The predefined tasks can be extremely useful for assessing patient conditions, and all can be incorporated into CareKit apps, saving developers a lot of effort.

ResearchKit also includes numerous charts: pie charts, line graphs, multiple-line graphs, discreet graphs, and discrete graphs with multiple points. It's quite possible for you to use these charts within a CareKit dashboard.

Consider having a look at the ResearchKit framework and familiarize yourself with the various features. Links are provided in the appendix.

HealthKit

We've covered incorporating HealthKit into CareKit apps with two examples. In the first instance you learned how to save data captured during assessment activities and then later you learned how to make uses of HealthKit data that did not originate from the example app into the Insights reports.

HealthKit data is stored securely and is a central database of a wide range of health data which, with the correct permissions granted by the user, can provide very useful information to a Care Team. The HealthKit store is also directly accessible from the Apple Watch.

For more information on HealthKit, go to `https://developer.apple.com/healthkit/`.

Notifications

iOS notifications alert users to useful information in your app. You've seen examples of this where you learned to send local notifications about scheduled activities in the ZombieCare app that can be viewed on an iPhone or an Apple Watch.

There is plenty of potential for using notifications. Apple gives one example where you might want to notify a user if they are taking a large number of steps, which was detected in your app, when they are supposed to be resting or recovering from surgery.

You can read more about local and remote notifications in Apple's guide at `https://developer.apple.com/library/ios/documentation/NetworkingInternet/Conceptual/RemoteNotificationsPG/Chapters/Introduction.html`.

Apple Watch

Chapter 8 introduced you to the Apple Watch, and you learned how to build a custom watchOS app that incorporated data from your CareKit app. Although a custom app can play a useful part in your solution, it's not always necessary because it can still receive notifications that are forwarded from a paired iPhone.

There are lots of other features of an Apple Watch you can take advantage of. The watch comes with numerous sensors and records large amounts of useful information, including activity summaries, step counts, heart rate samples, and more. This data is all synced to HealthKit, which can be accessed on the iPhone app.

To explore the features available on Apple watchOS, go to `https://developer.apple.com/library/watchos/documentation/General/Conceptual/WatchKitProgrammingGuide/index.html`.

Motion Sensors

Core Motion is an Apple framework that lets developers access data from an iOS device's motion coprocessor. This framework enables you to determine whether a user is stationary, walking, running, cycling, or even driving.

ResearchKit has a number of tasks that use the Core Motion framework, so look for suitable tasks there first—otherwise, consider accessing the framework yourself with your own custom tasks.

Asynchronous APIs

CareKit uses asynchronous reads and writes to the Care Plan Store. When reading or writing data, work is placed on a background thread, after which methods return immediately. When results are ready they are returned in completion handlers.

A number of options are available to developers for working with background threads, including GCD and closures, dispatch queues, native threads, and NSOperation Queues. It's worth exploring these options if you have no experience with them so that your app can be responsive and you will be able to better understand how CareKit makes use of background threads.

For further information on concurrency programming, see the appropriate links in the appendix. You may also find it useful to watch the video on "Advanced NSOperations" from WWDC 2015 (`https://developer.apple.com/videos/play/wwdc2015/226/`).

Networking and Remote Services

In the example ZombieCare app, a mock service was used to load the Care Plan. This example was used to demonstrate how you might architect an app that requires information from a remote service. In a real production application, you may be required to download medical records, Care Plans, and other information from remote servers.

I have included a new node service you can run as an example of a remote service (albeit on your local machine). Download the careplanserver source code folder and follow the readme instructions to install it and run it on your local machine.

Open the source code from the /project_folder/chapter_09 and you will find a new service called TestService has been added to the project. This version of the project has been modified to load the TestService by default (see the `ZCServiceProvider.` `userbackendType()` method).

If you run this version of the project, resources will be loaded from the service and not the local resource in the app bundle. This simply demonstrates an alternative method of loading data from a remote HTTP resource. The test service is still just returning a full Care Plan in JSON format but is easily extendable to be a fully RESTful service.

If you're interested in following the development of a new fully RESTful Care Plan service, you can register at `http://catalystcare.co`. Apple also provides APIs for networking technologies. Refer to the appendix for URL session programming guides.

Summary

In this chapter you've read about just a few of the iOS frameworks and technologies available to developers building CareKit applications.

There are a lot more. And in addition to Apple's iOS SDK, there are plenty of third-party libraries and products (open source and commercial) that you might be able to use in your CareKit apps to give the best features and user experience. If you're looking for further resources, consider looking at the Cocoapods or Carthage package managers, and at some point soon, the Swift Package Manager.

Resources

This appendix lists useful tools and links for building iOS and CareKit applications. It provides various resources and tools that you might find useful when building CareKit applications. Although not an exhaustive list, it should give you a head start if you're new to iOS development.

Apple Documentation

CareKit

http://carekit.org/docs/docs/Overview/Overview.html

ResearchKit

http://researchkit.org/docs/docs/Overview/GuideOverview.html

HealthKit

https://developer.apple.com/healthkit/

iOS Human Interface Guidelines

https://developer.apple.com/ios/human-interface-guidelines/

App Development Tutorial (Swift)

https://developer.apple.com/library/ios/referencelibrary/GettingStarted/DevelopiOSAppsSwift/index.html

© Christopher Baxter 2016
C. Baxter, *Beginning CareKit Development*, DOI 10.1007/978-1-4842-2226-3

ViewController Programming Guide for iOS

https://developer.apple.com/library/ios/featuredarticles/
ViewControllerPGforiPhoneOS/

Local and Remote Notification Programming Guide

https://developer.apple.com/library/ios/documentation/NetworkingInternet/
Conceptual/RemoteNotificationsPG/Chapters/Introduction.html

Core Motion Framework Reference

https://developer.apple.com/library/ios/documentation/CoreMotion/Reference/
CoreMotion_Reference/index.html

Concurrency Programming Guide

https://developer.apple.com/library/ios/documentation/General/Conceptual/
ConcurrencyProgrammingGuide/Introduction/Introduction.html

Networking with NSURLSession

https://developer.apple.com/videos/play/wwdc2015/711/NSURLSession
Programming Guide
https://developer.apple.com/library/ios/documentation/Cocoa/Conceptual/
URLLoadingSystem/URLLoadingSystem.html

Apple Watch Programming Guide

https://developer.apple.com/library/watchos/documentation/General/
Conceptual/WatchKitProgrammingGuide/index.html

App Extension Programming Guide

https://developer.apple.com/library/ios/documentation/General/Conceptual/
ExtensibilityPG/

Apple Open Source Repositories

CareKit Repository

https://github.com/carekit-apple/CareKit

ResearchKit Repository

https://github.com/ResearchKit/ResearchKit

Source Code Version control Systems

Github

https://github.com

Bitbucket

https://bitbucket.org

Package Managers

CocoaPods

https://cocoapods.org

Carthage

https://github.com/Carthage/Carthage

Swift Package Manager

https://swift.org/package-manager/

Index

© Christopher Baxter 2016
C. Baxter, *Beginning CareKit Development*, DOI 10.1007/978-1-4842-2226-3

■ D, E, F, G

▨ Z

Get the eBook for only $4.99!

Why limit yourself?

Now you can take the weightless companion with you wherever you go and access your content on your PC, phone, tablet, or reader.

Since you've purchased this print book, we are happy to offer you the eBook for just $4.99.

Convenient and fully searchable, the PDF version enables you to easily find and copy code—or perform examples by quickly toggling between instructions and applications.

To learn more, go to http://www.apress.com/us/shop/companion or contact support@apress.com.

Printed in the United States
By Bookmasters